WASTE NOT
WANT NOT

WASTE NOT
WANT NOT

Helen McCully

RANDOM HOUSE
NEW YORK

Illustrations by Mel Klapholz

Copyright © 1975 by Helen McCully

All rights reserved under International and Pan-American Copyright Conventions. Published in the United States by Random House, Inc., New York, and simultaneously in Canada by Random House of Canada Limited, Toronto.

Library of Congress Cataloging in Publication Data

McCully, Helen.
Waste not want not.
Includes index.
1. Cookery. I. Title.
TX652.M2   641.5   75-10287
ISBN 0-394-49549-7

Manufactured in the United States of America

24689753

CONTENTS

INTRODUCTION

When I was growing up in Nova Scotia, I often heard my father protest that he wouldn't think of eating leftovers. Little did he know that the wonderful soups and stews and creamed dishes we had were models of cooking with bits and pieces left from an earlier meal. Susan, our cook, wouldn't have dreamed of wasting food. Our kitchen was bountiful, but it was also practical. To my father, however, and to all too many fathers who were well off, eating leftovers meant that you couldn't afford better, and it was a matter of pride for the head of the house to provide the best. This kind of vanity has never troubled the households of France, where thriftiness is a virtue and the waste of a crumb of good food would be considered folly. The same is true in most other countries of Europe and elsewhere in the world. They've all seen too much history.

Why are Americans so wasteful? Because we're young? Because we've had too much? Because we're too lazy? Because we lack imagination? It's clear that our bad habits are coming home to roost. We are faced with shortages in all parts of our economy, and we can no longer take our ribs of beef and porterhouse steaks for granted. In recent years we have experienced a shortage of grain and meat, and we have seen such humble items as rice, dried beans and sugar soaring in price. This is just the beginning, and it is not a moment too soon for cooks in this land to settle down and learn to use what the French call *les restes*.

It may be a matter of expediency for many housewives, but I'd like to convince you in this book that serving your family a meal of leftovers is not the sign of a fallen woman. It's smart. It can give you the psychological lift of doing a good deed. And if you use your imagination it can really be fun. Can you think of anything nicer to eat than a big tureen of heart-warming pea soup made with a leftover ham bone and split peas? Flaky pastry fingers to serve with soup or salads made from a handful of leftover pastry? A delicate rice pudding made with leftover rice, perfumed with orange and lemon juice? A spinach soufflé puffed to fabulous heights, made with leftover spinach and leftover egg whites? A rich gingerbread made with soured (not commercial) cream? The list is endless, the culinary profits fantastic.

You will find that this book is arranged according to the leftover ingredient you might have on hand. What do you do with egg whites, for example, after you have used the yolks for a Hollandaise? Look in the chapter on eggs for ways of using anywhere from one leftover white to ten. You will also find suggestions for using the yolks. The meat chapters include recipes for slices of leftover roast, diced meat, ground meat, and finally even the bare or nearly bare bones. You might be surprised to learn that apple parings have a second life, as well as stale beer, cold coffee and wilted salad.

This is not only a book about leftovers, however, because to "waste not" you must prevent the spoilage of either raw or cooked foods. Therefore you will find information on the proper storage of food in your refrigerator or freezer, as recommended by the U.S.D.A., the National Livestock and Meat Board, the National Broiler Council, and the Western Fruit and Vegetable Growers Association. You will also find a great many special tips—how to keep carrots alive and well, how to stockpile your chicken livers and other giblets, how to freeze citrus peels, heavy cream, and egg whites; how to salvage sour milk and hardened brown sugar. Charts containing weights and measures and standard equivalents are also included at the back of the book.

As the mother of a friend of ours used to say in an earlier generation, "Nothing gets thrown out of this kitchen except the coffee grounds." It's a challenge to live up to. We're returning to many of the virtues practiced by our ancestors, like growing our own vegetables and baking our own bread, so it makes sense to return to their reverence for the food that blessed their tables. In the wise words of the *Old Cook's Almanac*, "A wasteful woman can throw out at the back door with a teaspoon more than a man can carry in at the front door with a shovel."

MEATS

Storing Meat

Fresh prepackaged meats should be stored, unopened, in their original wrappings in the coldest part of the refrigerator, the meat storing compartment or in the freezer (in this case, add another layer of freezer wrap). Meats that are *not* prepackaged should be stored in the refrigerator loosely wrapped to permit some air circulation. *Slight* drying increases keeping quality. FREEZERS MUST MAINTAIN ZERO F. OR LOWER TEMPERATURE. I recommend keeping thermometers in both refrigerator and freezer.

MAXIMUM MEAT STORAGE TIME*

MEAT	REFRIGERATOR (36° to 40° F.)	FREEZER (at 0° F. or lower)
Beef (fresh)	2 to 4 days	6 to 12 months
Veal (fresh)	2 to 4 days	6 to 9 months
Pork (fresh)	2 to 4 days	3 to 6 months
Lamb (fresh)	2 to 4 days	6 to 9 months
Ground beef, veal and lamb	1 to 2 days	3 to 4 months
Ground pork	1 to 2 days	1 to 3 months
Variety meats	1 to 2 days	3 to 4 months
Luncheon meats	1 week	not recommended
Sausage, fresh pork	1 week	60 days
Sausage, smoked	3 to 7 days	not recommended

* From the 1974 edition of *Lessons on Meat,* published by the National Livestock and Meat Board.

MEAT	REFRIGERATOR (36° to 40° F.)	FREEZER (at 0° F. or lower)
Sausage, dry and semi-dry (unsliced)	2 to 3 weeks	not recommended
Frankfurters	4 to 5 days	1 month
Bacon	5 to 7 days	1 month
Smoked ham, whole	1 week	60 days
Ham slices	3 to 4 days	60 days
Beef, corned	1 week	2 weeks
Leftover cooked meat	4 to 5 days	2 to 3 months
Meat pies (cooked)	—	3 months
Swiss steak (cooked)	—	3 months
Stews (cooked)	—	3 to 4 months
Prepared meat dinners	—	2 to 6 months
Gravy and meat broths	1 to 2 days	2 to 3 months

Marinating Meat

Marinades were originally simple brines for preserving fish which accounts for the name, derived from the French word *mariner*, meaning to put in salt water. Today, marinades are used to tenderize and flavor meat and are usually composed of oil (vegetable, peanut or olive) and acid (vinegar and/or lemon juice and/or wine) and herbs and/or spices. However, it is a good idea to remember the original purpose of marinades, which is preservation. So if you have some meat that is slightly "high" or may not survive until you get around to cooking it, you can "save it" by marinating it and thus prolong its life as much as four or five days.

The type of marinade you use and the length of time the meat is marinated depends, of course, on the dish you are ultimately going to prepare. You can use marinated meat in almost all the ways you would use fresh meat. If you are baking or sautéing, dry the meat first.

Broadly speaking, you should allow about 1 cup of marinade for every pound of meat. Unless the meat is of gargantuan size, I use plastic bags for marinating, which I find much more satisfactory than pans or bowls. Add the meat to the bag, then the marinade, squeeze out all air and tie tightly. Place the whole thing in a pan in case of leakage and turn the bag as often as possible so the meat is well soaked. The length of time runs from a few hours up to as much as several days, depending on the recipe.

Note: Marinades can be kept 4 to 5 days, strained, bottled and refrigerated. To use again add a little fresh wine or vinegar or lemon juice. If you wish to keep the marinade longer, freeze in suitable container.

Here are several marinades for meat or game.

QUICK MARINADE

Salt
Freshly ground pepper
6 or 7 green onion bulbs
  (scallions), peeled and
  minced fine
1 sprig fresh thyme or good
  pinch dried

4 to 5 sprigs parsley
1 bay leaf
½ cup vegetable or peanut oil
½ cup lemon juice, strained
  (about 2 lemons)
½ cup wine vinegar

Season the meat with salt and pepper. Place in a plastic bag, add all remaining ingredients, squeeze out all air and tie tightly. Place in a pan in case of leakage and marinate 12 to 24 hours, turning frequently, so meat gets well soaked. Makes 1½ cups.

COOKED MARINADE

2 tablespoons butter or
    margarine
1 carrot, washed and sliced
1 yellow onion, peeled and
    sliced
4 or 5 sprigs parsley
1 bay leaf
Big pinch thyme
1 clove garlic, crushed and
    peeled

1 cup water
2 tablespoons vegetable or
    peanut oil
½ cup dry white or red
    jug wine
4 tablespoons tarragon
    vinegar
4 or 5 peppercorns

Melt the butter or margarine in a skillet. Add the vegetables
and herbs. Cook for a few minutes to soften them, stirring
frequently. Add the liquids and peppercorns and simmer until
reduced to about one-third. Allow to cool. Place the meat in
a plastic bag. Add the marinade, squeeze out all air and tie
securely. Place in a pan in case of leakage. Marinate for 24 hours,
turning the bag often so the meat is well soaked. Makes about
2 cups.

UNCOOKED MARINADE

Salt
Freshly ground pepper
3 yellow onions, peeled and
    sliced thin
3 carrots, washed and sliced
    thin
2 cloves
1 bay leaf
1 clove garlic, crushed and
    peeled

10 peppercorns
4 or 5 sprigs parsley
2 cups dry white (for fish or
    poultry) or red (for meat)
    jug wine
½ cup vegetable or peanut oil
¼ cup wine vinegar

Season the meat with salt and pepper. Place in a plastic bag with all the vegetables and seasonings. Mix the wine, oil and vinegar together and add to the bag. Squeeze out all air and tie securely. Place in a pan in case of leakage. Marinate for 2 to 3 days, turning frequently. Makes about 3 cups.

Gravy

Don't Leave the Flavor in the Pan

Deglaze the roasting pan or skillet after you've cooked meat by adding water, broth, or wine. Bring to a simmer, scraping the sides and bottom of the pan to incorporate all the coagulated juices. Use these good salvaged juices in making gravy, soups, broth, stews.

Save the Gravy

After the meat has done the honors as a roast, save any leftover gravy or pan juices and add to stews or hash.

Reheating Cooked Meat in a Sauce or Gravy

The sauce should first be slightly warmed, the meat added to it and the whole brought up to the boiling point. That's it. Cooked meat put into boiling sauce will toughen and shrink, and the flavor of the sauce will not penetrate the meat.

Fats

Rendered Fat

Fat from beef, pork (bacon), chicken, goose, and duck can all be rendered and used for cooking. Lamb and mutton fat, because of their distinctive flavor, are used only with great discretion. Bacon and pork fats should be stored separately, but others can be mixed. Always keep rendered fat refrigerated or frozen.

To Render Fat

Cut the fat into small dice, place in a heavy saucepan with enough cold water to cover. Bring to a boil and continue to boil until all the water has evaporated, the remaining liquid is clear and the pieces of fat have browned lightly and shriveled. Stir frequently during this period. When cool, strain and pour into a jar.

Clarifying Used Fats

Fat that has been used in deep-fat frying can be reused if it doesn't carry the flavor from a previous frying—fish, for example.

To clarify, add a few slices of potato to the fat and reheat slowly, stirring occasionally. Strain, bottle and refrigerate. Obviously, there comes a point when the fat should be discarded and you should start with *fresh* fat.

Meat Bones and Broth

When you buy meat, any meat, make sure the butcher gives you the bones he may have trimmed away. After all, you're paying for them. Regardless of the kind of bones (beef, veal, lamb, pork, chicken, game, duck, goose), once you have removed all the fat and the skin, they can be used to make a savory broth. This can then be used in any dish, no matter what specific type of broth the recipe calls for. For example, you can use beef broth with lamb without being able to tell the difference. The two exceptions are ham and fish. The broths do taste of the original source.

So using the Basic Broth recipe for meat and poultry as guides, make the most of all and any bones that come your way (including cooked bones from roasts and chops) and always, unfailingly, ask the butcher for trimmings and bones when he prepares your meat.

A further point, any broth can always be concentrated, or to put it another way, made stronger by reducing (cooking it down). Something worth knowing when you need a rich concentrate to add to a sauce or a particular dish.

BASIC MEAT BROTH

ANY LEFTOVER BONES FROM BEEF, VEAL OR LAMB WITH BITS OF MEAT CLINGING TO THEM (ABOUT 2 POUNDS), COOKED OR UNCOOKED*
2 large yellow onions, peeled and sliced
2 carrots, washed and chopped
2 ribs celery, chopped

1 bouquet garni tied in a cheesecloth bag:
4 to 6 sprigs parsley, big pinch thyme, 1 bay leaf, 2 cloves, 6 to 8 peppercorns, 1 clove garlic, crushed and peeled
2 teaspoons tomato paste
Cold water to cover

Preheat oven to 450°.

Place the bones, onions, carrots and celery in a roasting pan and bake, uncovered, for about 15 minutes or until they are very well browned. Take care not to scorch the vegetables. If they seem to be browning too much, lift from the pan to a soup kettle. Once the bones are brown, place them in the kettle with the vegetables and all remaining ingredients. Bring to a boil very, very slowly, skimming off any scum that rises to the surface. Reduce heat and simmer, covered, for 2 to 3 hours or until you have a good strong flavor. Skim regularly.

Strain through a coarse sieve lined with several layers of dampened cheesecloth. Chill and lift off any fat that has congealed on the surface. Do not season until you are ready to use the broth.

Broth should be refrigerated as soon as it is taken off the stove. To keep for several days, place in a tightly sealed jar or freeze in suitable freezer containers. We recommend storing in small amounts—1 pint or less.

---

* If you use a leg of lamb, break it apart at the joint so it will fit into your soup kettle.

BROWN SAUCE

Known as a "mother" sauce, Brown Sauce is the foundation for innumerable classic sauces but is also used to thicken and enrich other sauces and gravies. Store in small quantities in the refrigerator, or freeze. It will keep up to ten days refrigerated; 2 to 3 months in the freezer.

3 to 4 POUNDS LEFTOVER
    BONES, CUT INTO SMALL
    PIECES
2 quarts boiling water
½ cup rendered meat fat
    (page 8) or vegetable
    oil
½ small yellow onion, peeled
    and diced
1 carrot, washed and diced
1 rib celery, diced

2 tablespoons all-purpose flour
1 bouquet garni tied in a
    cheesecloth bag:
    3 bay leaves, 1 teaspoon
    thyme, 12 sprigs parsley,
    1 teaspoon peppercorns,
    1 small clove garlic,
    crushed and peeled
Salt
Freshly ground pepper

Preheat oven to 400°.

Wash the beef bones and place in a shallow baking pan. Bake until they take on a rich dark brown color, stirring frequently. Once brown, place bones in a kettle and add 2 quarts of boiling water. Bring to a boil, reduce heat and simmer until you have about 1½ quarts of liquid.

In another kettle place the fat with the vegetables and cook, stirring often, until the vegetables are golden brown. Stir in the flour until smooth and continue to cook until the mixture is a deep brown. Stir occasionally.

Strain the contents from the second kettle through a fine sieve, pressing the vegetables with a rubber spatula to extract all the juices. Pour the juices into the first kettle. Add the bouquet garni. Bring to a boil. Skim off any scum. Reduce heat and simmer for 2 hours, skimming off fat and scum as necessary. If sauce seems to thicken too much, add more liquid (broth, if you have some, or boiling water). When finished, the sauce should be thick enough to coat a spoon lightly. Taste here for seasoning. It will need both salt and pepper. Makes about 4 cups. Refrigerate immediately until cold. Then skim off any fat.

LENTIL SOUP

This soup is perfectly delicious with knackwurst or hotdogs, spread with Dijon or Düsseldorf mustard. Serve about 3 pieces in each soup plate.

2 cups dry lentils
2½ quarts water
LEFTOVER BEEF, LAMB OR
    PORK ROAST BONES
*1 large yellow onion, peeled
    and minced*
2 carrots, washed and minced
2 ribs celery, with leaves, sliced

*1 clove garlic, crushed and
    peeled*
2 teaspoons oregano
2 teaspoons salt
Freshly ground black pepper
¼ teaspoon ground cloves
2 bay leaves
⅓ cup sherry or Madeira

Pick over the lentils because sometimes you'll find odds and ends such as weed seed, dried soil (known as "dobie"), even tiny stones. Then put them into a colander under cold running water.

Place in a large kettle with 2½ quarts water. Add the bones and all other ingredients except the wine. Bring to a boil, reduce heat, cover and simmer for about 2 hours or until the lentils are soft. Skim off any scum that rises to the surface. Once cooked, remove and discard the bones and bay leaves. Purée the beans with a little liquid, a small amount at a time, in an electric food processor or an electric blender. Return to the kettle and stir in the wine. Makes about 2 quarts.

WHITE BEAN SOUP MADE WITH LEFTOVER BONES

3 quarts water
2 cups (one 16-ounce package)
  dry white beans
LEFTOVER BEEF, VEAL, PORK
  OR LAMB BONES
2 large onions, peeled
1 bouquet garni tied in a
  cheesecloth bag:
  2 or 3 sprigs parsley, 1 bay
  leaf, 1 teaspoon dried
  thyme, 6 to 8 peppercorns

2 or 3 large cloves garlic,
  crushed and peeled
Salt
2 tablespoons butter
4 green onion bulbs, peeled
  and chopped fine
2 ripe tomatoes, or 2 to 3
  canned Italian tomatoes,
  chopped
Freshly ground pepper
Minced parsley

Bring the water to a boil. Meanwhile, wash the beans and pick them over. Once the water has reached the boiling point, add the beans and bring to a boil. Boil 2 minutes. Take off the heat, cover, and let stand for 1 hour. Drain. (Beans can be soaked overnight in cold water rather than prepared by this quick method.)

Place the bones in a casserole. Add the beans, onions, bouquet garni, the garlic and a good tablespoon of salt. Cover with cold water. If you have a little red wine sitting in a bottle doing nothing, add it, too. Bring up to a boil. Reduce heat to a simmer, cover and cook about an hour or until the beans are soft but still shapely. Lift the onions from the casserole and chop. Discard bouquet garni.

Melt the butter in a heavy skillet. Add the chopped onions, green onions and tomatoes. Mix well. Cook over moderate heat, stirring occasionally, for about 15 minutes.

Lift the bones from the casserole. Cut off any meat and add to the beans. Discard the bones. Stir in the vegetables and taste for seasoning. It will undoubtedly need salt and pepper. Bring up to a boil. Serve in hot soup plates with a garnish of minced parsley. Makes 4 generous portions.

BEAN SOUP WITH MEAT BROTH

1½ cups dry beans, kidney,   1 thick slice salt pork, cubed
  black, great northern,   1 teaspoon dry mustard
  pinto or lima   2 tablespoons molasses
1½ CUPS MEAT BROTH   2 tablespoons tomato paste
  (page 10), HEATED   1 tablespoon vinegar
1 large onion, peeled and   Salt
  diced   Freshly ground pepper

Wash and soak the beans overnight or use this quick method:
Bring measured amount of water to boiling point (allow
3 quarts of water to 1 pound of beans). Add the washed beans.
Bring to a boil again and boil *exactly 2 minutes.* Take off the
heat, cover and allow to stand for 1 hour.

Drain beans. Place in a saucepan, add remaining ingredients. Cover and cook until beans are very tender when pressed
between thumb and forefinger. Drain the beans, reserving
broth, and purée them, a small amount at a time, in an electric
food processor or blender. Combine the purée with the broth
and bring to a boil. Taste for seasoning. Makes in the neigh-
borhood of 10 to 12 cups.

ONION SOUP

John W. Iliff of New Bern, N.C., a splendid cook, uses fish
broth to make his onion soup, calling it "Onion Ocean Soup."

5 tablespoons butter or   1½ teaspoons salt
  margarine   6 CUPS MEAT BROTH (page 10)
2 tablespoons peanut or   1 cup dry red wine or port
  vegetable oil   French bread, toasted
5 medium yellow onions,   Grated Parmesan cheese
  peeled and sliced thin

Heat the butter and oil in a heavy saucepan. Add the onions
and cook until soft and lightly colored. Add the salt, broth

and wine. Bring to a boil and boil for 5 minutes or so. Place a piece of toast in each soup plate. Add the soup and sprinkle with cheese. Serves about 6.

CABBAGE SOUP WITH RED WINE

¼ pound salt pork, finely   *Salt*
    diced   *Freshly ground pepper*
1 small cabbage, finely   *1 cup dry red jug wine,*
    shredded   *heated*
5 CUPS MEAT BROTH *(page 10)*   *Croutons (page 197)*

Place the pork in a heavy saucepan and fry over moderate heat until golden. Lift from the pan with a slotted spoon and set aside. Add the cabbage and soften in the pork fat, stirring constantly. *Do not brown.* Add the broth. Bring to a boil, reduce heat, and simmer for 15 minutes. Taste for seasoning.

Take 1½ cups of the soup and purée in a blender or electric food processor. Pour back into the saucepan, add the pork bits and bring the soup to a boil. Stir in the hot wine.

Serve in hot soup plates with croutons. Serves about 6.

MUSHROOM AND TOMATO SOUP

5 tablespoons butter or   *5 tablespoons peanut or*
    margarine   *vegetable oil*
¼ pound (about 12) fresh   *2 cups tomato purée*
    button mushrooms, sliced   *1 clove garlic, crushed and*
    thin   *peeled*
4 CUPS MEAT BROTH   *1 teaspoon powdered fennel*
    (page 10), HEATED   *Salt*
2 tablespoons vermicelli   *Freshly ground pepper*
                                      Croutons (page 197)

Melt 2 tablespoons of the butter in a heavy saucepan. Add the mushrooms and cook over moderate heat for 2 minutes. Pour in the hot broth, then add the vermicelli and simmer for 10 minutes.

Melt the remaining butter with the oil in a saucepan. Add the tomato purée, garlic and fennel. Cook 10 minutes. Season to taste with salt and freshly ground pepper. Combine with the mushroom soup and bring to a boil.

Serve with buttered croutons to 6.

MME. FERNANDE ERNOULT'S SAUCE PIQUANTE

A sprightly sauce to serve with leftover boiled beef or tongue, hot or cold.

2 tablespoons butter or margarine
3 or 4 green onion bulbs, peeled and minced
1 cup water
2 tablespoons all-purpose flour

2 CUPS MEAT BROTH (*page 10*)
Kitchen Bouquet
Wine vinegar
Sour gherkins, coarsely chopped

Melt the butter in a heavy saucepan. Add the onions and the cup of water. Bring to a boil and cook until all the water has boiled away and the onions are tender. Add more water if necessary. Stir in the flour until smooth and cook, stirring constantly, for about 3 or 4 minutes. Add broth and beat with a wire whip. Bring up to a boil, reduce heat somewhat and cook until the sauce has thickened lightly. Add a dash of Kitchen Bouquet to give it a good rich color. Then add a generous dash of vinegar to give the sauce a nice bite. Finally, stir in a handful or so of gherkins. Makes about 2 cups.

Meat Salads and Sandwiches

MEAT SANDWICHES
MAKE A MEAL

Leftover steak, roast beef, lamb or pork, sliced thin, makes an
especially delicious sandwich when made with French or Italian
bread, seasoned butter (see below) and served with pickles (dill
or sweet) and thinly sliced sweet onions tossed in a Vinaigrette
Sauce, page 229. A glass of red jug wine would not come amiss.

Mustard Butter: Soften as much butter as you think you'll
need and stir in prepared mustard to taste.

Garlic Butter: Crush, peel and mince 4 cloves of garlic and
mix with 6 tablespoons (¾ stick) softened butter, salt and
freshly ground pepper to taste.

Anchovy Butter: To 8 tablespoons (1 stick) softened butter,
add anchovy paste to taste.

MEAT SALAD

Marinate thin slices of steak or diced roast beef, lamb, or pork
in Sauce Vinaigrette, page 229, along with a little finely chopped
onion and parsley for a couple of hours. Serve on lettuce with a
garnish of gherkins and, if you like, sliced hard-cooked eggs.

Beef

BEEF HASH

2 CUPS GROUND LEFTOVER
   BEEF (OR CORNED BEEF,
   LAMB OR PORK)
2 cups diced cooked potatoes
2 tablespoons butter or
   margarine or meat drippings
2 medium yellow onions,
   peeled and grated
½ cup meat broth (page 10),
   leftover gravy or cream

About 10 sprigs parsley,
   minced
½ cup fresh bread crumbs
   (page 197)
1 egg
Salt
Freshly ground black pepper
1 tablespoon Worcestershire
   sauce

Combine meat and potatoes in a large bowl. Set aside momentarily.

Melt the fat in a large heavy skillet. Add the grated onions (both juice and pulp). Cook over moderate heat, stirring frequently, until lightly browned. Add to the meat and potatoes. Add all other ingredients, and mix together with your hands. Lift into the skillet and cook over moderate heat, stirring constantly until the mixture seems to leave the sides of the pan. It should be of the right consistency to make into patties. If too thin, add a few more bread crumbs; if too thick, broth or cream. Spoon into a bowl, cover, and refrigerate until firm.

To cook, shape into flat cakes rather on the thick side. Brown on both sides in melted butter or margarine or drippings. Serve with chili sauce or catsup. Makes 6 to 8 patties.

SAVORY RICE AND BEEF
CASSEROLE

3 tablespoons butter or
   margarine
2 medium yellow onions,
   peeled and sliced thin
1½ CUPS GROUND OR
   CHOPPED LEFTOVER BEEF,
   LAMB, OR VEAL
1 cup gravy or meat broth
   (page 10), seasoned with
   rosemary

1 clove garlic, crushed, peeled
   and minced
2 cups cooked rice
3 eggs, lightly beaten
8 to 10 sprigs parsley, minced
Salt
Freshly ground pepper

Preheat oven to 350°.

Butter well a 5- or 6-cup casserole that has a cover and set aside.

Melt the remaining butter in a heavy skillet. Add onions and sauté until lightly browned. Combine with all remaining ingredients, seasoning with salt and pepper to taste. Spoon into the casserole, cover, and bake for 25 minutes. Should serve 4 to 5.

MEAT SAUCE FOR SPAGHETTI

1 clove garlic, crushed, peeled
   and minced
1 medium yellow onion,
   peeled and chopped fine
Few sprigs parsley, minced
1 CUP FINELY CHOPPED LEFT-
   OVER BEEF, LAMB OR VEAL
2 tablespoons butter or
   margarine

2 tablespoons olive or
   vegetable oil or half and
   half
¼ teaspoon oregano
½ teaspoon salt
Several twists of the
   peppermill
½ cup dry white wine
Parmesan cheese

Combine the vegetables, parsley and meat. Heat the butter and oil in a heavy skillet. Add the meat mixture and cook, stirring, until the onion is soft. Stir in the seasonings and wine. Bring up to a boil. Reduce heat and simmer 10 minutes, giving the mixture an occasional stir.

Serve hot over freshly cooked spaghetti with freshly grated Parmesan cheese on the side. Serves 4.

MEAT-STUFFED CABBAGE

1 CUP GROUND LEFTOVER BEEF OR OTHER MEAT	½ cup cooked rice
1 egg	1 teaspoon dried thyme
1 small yellow onion, peeled and minced	Salt
3 tablespoons butter or margarine, melted	Freshly ground pepper
	1 medium head cabbage
	Thin Sauce Béchamel (page 230)

Mix together all ingredients, except cabbage and sauce, adding salt and pepper to taste. Set aside.

Cut out the center of the cabbage, making a cavity large enough to hold the stuffing. In a saucepan, cover cabbage head with boiling salted water and boil for 10 minutes. Remove from water and drain upside down.

Stuff the cabbage. Tie it securely in a triple thickness of cheesecloth. Lower it into boiling salted water in a pan slightly larger than the cabbage. Simmer 35 to 40 minutes.

Before serving, lift the cabbage to a rack to allow it to drain. When it seems to have lost all liquid, remove the cheesecloth and place on a heated serving platter.

Serve with Sauce Béchamel to 4 or 5.

MEAT-STUFFED ONIONS

These make an attractive luncheon or supper dish. Sweet green peppers (seeded, ribs removed and parboiled for 5 minutes) can be substituted for the onions, in which case, add 1 small onion, sautéed in 2 tablespoons of butter, to the filling. Bake the peppers for 30 minutes.

4 large yellow onions, peeled
  (don't cut off ends)
1 cup soft bread crumbs
1 tablespoon tomato paste
1 CUP GROUND LEFTOVER MEAT
1 clove garlic, crushed and
  peeled

2 tablespoons butter, melted
1 teaspoon dried thyme
Salt
Freshly ground pepper
Grated cheese

Preheat oven to 375° (350° for stuffed peppers).

Drop the onions into boiling salted water and parboil for 10 minutes. Scoop out the centers. Mix together all remaining ingredients, except the cheese, with salt and pepper to taste. Fill the onions and sprinkle with grated cheese.

Place in a baking dish or casserole with a little water in the bottom of the dish to keep the onions from scorching. Bake 30 to 40 minutes or until tender.

CHINESE STIR-FRIED MEAT

This is a wonderful way to serve sliced leftover meat that isn't
too well done. If you haven't got a wok just use a big skillet.

SLICED LEFTOVER BEEF, LAMB,
   PORK OR VEAL
1 tablespoon cornstarch
   dissolved in 3 tablespoons
   soy sauce
½ teaspoon fresh ginger or
   ¼ teaspoon dried

1 tablespoon sherry
1 clove garlic, peeled,
   crushed and minced
Sugar to taste
Peanut or vegetable oil for
   frying

Cut meat into very thin strips. Combine all remaining ingredients except the oil and coat meat with mixture. Heat oil
in a wok or frying pan over moderate to high heat and add
the meat and liquid. Keep tossing meat in pan until it is
piping hot, but not overcooked. Delicious with hot rice.

BEEF WITH ONION SAUCE

3 tablespoons butter or
   margarine
4 large yellow onions, peeled
   and sliced thin
1 tablespoon all-purpose flour

1 cup meat broth (page 10)
Salt
Freshly ground pepper
½ teaspoon wine vinegar
LEFTOVER BEEF, SLICED

Preheat oven to 300°.

Heat the butter in a heavy skillet. Add the onions and
sauté until brown. Sprinkle with the flour and cook, stirring,
until the mixture froths, about 3 minutes. Stir in the broth
and bring to a boil, whipping constantly. Season with salt
and pepper. Add the vinegar and simmer 15 minutes.

Arrange the beef on a platter and coat with the sauce.
Place in the oven just long enough to heat the meat—20 to 25
minutes.

LEFTOVER POT ROAST

Combined with Ratatouille (page 183), you can turn leftover pot roast into a most unusual and delicious casserole. The number of servings and the size casserole you use will depend on how much leftover meat you have.

Ratatouille (page 183)   *Swiss cheese, grated*
LEFTOVER POT ROAST, SLICED

Preheat oven to 350°.

Start with a layer of the ratatouille, add a layer of cold sliced pot roast, and continue to fill a casserole layer by layer. Cover and bake for 25 minutes or until the ratatouille is bubbling. Sprinkle the top with grated Swiss cheese and cook another 10 minutes. Serve with hot rice.

BEEF PIE WITH BISCUIT CRUST

3 tablespoons butter or
  margarine
2 medium yellow onions,
  peeled and sliced thin
½ cup water
2 CUPS DICED LEFTOVER BEEF
Salt
½ cup chili sauce

1 cup gravy or Brown Sauce
  (page 11)
10 to 12 button mushrooms,
  sliced thin (optional)
Biscuit dough, see below
10 to 12 sprigs parsley,
  minced

Preheat oven to 425°.

Melt half the butter in a heavy skillet. Add the onions and ½ cup of water. Cook over moderate heat until the water has boiled away and the onions are soft. Combine with the beef and season with salt to taste. Stir in the chili sauce, beef gravy and mushrooms. Spoon into a 1-quart casserole, piling it somewhat higher in the center.

Make up the biscuit dough. On a lightly floured pastry cloth roll out dough about ¼-inch thick and two inches larger than the top of casserole.

Roll up on the rolling pin, center over the casserole and unroll. With a small sharp knife trim the dough even with the edge of the dish. Press the dough against the edge with your thumb. Finish by pressing it again with the tines of a fork.

Bake for 15 minutes. Reduce heat to 350° and cook another 5 to 6 minutes longer. Serves 4.

Cole slaw makes a good companion.

Biscuit Dough

1 cup all-purpose flour
2 teaspoons baking powder
¼ teaspoon salt

4 tablespoons vegetable
    shortening
10 to 12 sprigs parsley, minced
⅓ cup cold milk (about)

Sift the flour with the baking powder and salt into a mixing bowl. Cut in the shortening with a pastry blender or two knives until the particles are like corn meal. Stir in the parsley. Mix in the milk slowly with a fork. Shape into a ball. Place on a lightly floured pastry cloth and knead for 2 or 3 minutes or until you have a smooth dough.

BOILED BEEF SALAD

2 CUPS CUBED LEFTOVER BEEF
2 cooked potatoes, peeled
    and diced
1 large yellow onion, peeled
    and minced
5 small sour pickles, chopped
2 ripe tomatoes, peeled,
    seeded and chopped

1 sweet pepper, seeded, ribs
    removed and chopped
½ clove garlic, crushed,
    peeled and minced
½ cup Sauce Vinaigrette
    (page 229)
6 to 8 sprigs parsley, minced

Combine all the ingredients except the sauce and parsley, mixing well with your hands. Toss lightly with the Sauce Vinaigrette and sprinkle with the minced parsley.

Chill a few hours in the refrigerator before serving. Makes 5 to 6 servings.

BEEF SOUFFLÉ

Butter or margarine
1½ cups thick Sauce
   Béchamel (page 230)*
½ cup shredded sharp
   Cheddar cheese (about 2
   ounces)
½ teaspoon marjoram
Dash cayenne

1 CUP FINELY CHOPPED
   LEFTOVER BEEF OR CORNED
   BEEF
6 to 8 sprigs parsley, minced
4 whole eggs, separated
Salt
Freshly ground pepper
2 extra egg whites

Preheat oven to 375°.

Butter a 2-quart soufflé dish, including the curve at the bottom, and coat with cheese, dumping any excess back into the measuring cup. Refrigerate.

Add the cheese to the Béchamel along with marjoram and cayenne. Place over moderate heat and stir until the cheese melts. Take off the heat and stir in the beef and parsley. Add the yolks, one at a time, beating hard with a wire whip after each addition. Taste here for seasoning. The soufflé can be prepared ahead to this point, set aside, sealed with plastic wrap.

Beat egg whites until they hold firm shiny peaks when the beater is held straight up. Beat about a third thoroughly into the meat mixture. Then pour over the remaining whites and fold in gently with a rubber spatula.

* Make the Sauce Béchamel in these proportions (see recipe): 3 tablespoons butter or margarine; 2 tablespoons flour; 1½ cups milk; salt and freshly ground pepper to taste.

Pour into the soufflé dish. Place on a baking sheet, bake for 25 to 30 minutes. Serve immediately.

DEVILED BEEF BONES

8 tablespoons (1 stick) butter
  or margarine, melted
2 tablespoons tarragon vinegar
2 to 2½ cups fine bread
  crumbs

8 to 10 RIBS FROM 3 ROASTS,
  THAWED*
Sauce Diable (page 234)

Combine the butter and vinegar in a flat dish. Place the crumbs on a large plate. Dip the ribs first in the butter mixture turning them to cover well. Then coat with the crumbs. Press the crumbs so they will stick well. Place on a broiling rack and broil 6 to 7 inches from the heat so they cook very slowly and don't burn. Keep a sharp eye out and turn them often so they are a rich brown all over. Broiling time in a preheated broiler is about 15 to 20 minutes. Serve with Sauce Diable.

* Freeze ribs from roasts, leaving enough meat on them to chew on.

Lamb

SAVORY LAMB

This nice homely dish makes a small amount of meat go quite a long way. The number of servings it makes will depend on how much leftover lamb you have.

Butter, drippings, margarine
  or vegetable oil
LEFTOVER ROAST LAMB, SLICED,
  ALL FAT CUT OFF
2 green onion bulbs, peeled
  and minced
1 clove garlic, crushed, peeled
  and minced

1 tablespoon all-purpose flour
1 tablespoon tomato purée
5 to 6 sprigs parsley, chopped
1 teaspoon paprika
Salt
Freshly ground pepper
1 cup meat broth (page 10)

Heat the fat in a heavy skillet. Add the lamb and brown quickly. Lift from the pan to paper towels. Add the green onions and garlic. Brown lightly, stirring. Stir in the flour until smooth. Then add the tomato purée, parsley, paprika, and salt and pepper to taste. Add the broth and cook, whipping, until the sauce thickens lightly. Place the sliced lamb in the sauce just long enough to heat through.

LAMB AND POTATO CASSEROLE
IN SPICY SAUCE

Butter or margarine
½ teaspoon ground allspice
2 yellow onions, peeled and
   chopped
2 cups meat broth (page 10)
2 tablespoons cornstarch
2 CUPS DICED LEFTOVER LAMB

3 or 4 sweet gherkins, minced
½ cup currant jelly
3 cooked potatoes, peeled
   and sliced
Salt
Freshly ground pepper

Preheat oven to 375°.

Butter a 2-quart casserole that can go to the table. Set aside.

Combine allspice and onions with the broth in a heavy saucepan and simmer until the onions are very soft. Mix the cornstarch with a little water to make a smooth paste. Stir into the sauce and continue to simmer, stirring until it has thickened lightly.

Arrange the lamb in the prepared casserole and cover with the gherkins and jelly. Add the sliced potatoes. Sprinkle with salt and pepper to taste. Pour the onion sauce over all and bake for about 30 minutes or until piping hot. Serves 4 to 6.

HASHED LAMB AND BANANAS

I took this recipe from a 1904 booklet published by the United Fruit Company. I find it charming.

"Fry a tablespoon of fine chopped onion in two tablespoonfuls of butter until softened but not browned; add a cup of stock or water and let simmer five minutes; then add two table-spoonfuls of currant jelly and a cup and a half of cold roast lamb freed from all skin and gristle and cut into cubes one-eighth of an inch in diameter. When thoroughly hot and the jelly melted, add a cup of sliced bananas, a teaspoonful of lemon juice, and if desired, a little claret or sherry, also salt and pepper as needed. Let stand over the flame a few moments to become very hot without boiling, then serve at once. This is particularly good served from the chafing dish. If a thick sauce be preferred, cook two level tablespoonfuls of flour in the butter before adding the liquid."

QUICK AND EASY MOUSSAKA

A simplified version of the famous Middle Eastern dish made with leftover lamb or beef.

3 medium eggplants
Salt
All-purpose flour
¼ cup vegetable, peanut or olive oil
1 to 2 yellow onions, peeled and sliced thin
2 cloves garlic, crushed, peeled, and minced
1 ripe tomato, peeled, seeded and chopped
3 tablespoons tomato paste

15 to 20 sprigs parsley, minced
½ cup water
1½ to 2 CUPS GROUND LEFTOVER LAMB OR BEEF
Salt
Freshly ground pepper
½ teaspoon ground cinnamon (optional)
1¼ cups medium Sauce Béchamel (page 230)
1 or 2 egg yolks

Preheat oven to 350°.

Cut the eggplant in ½-inch slices. Sprinkle both sides generously with salt. Place in a bowl and allow to stand for about 30 minutes. Cover with cold water and allow to stand another 10 minutes. Squeeze out the water and blot with paper towels to dry. Coat lightly with flour.

Heat the oil in a heavy skillet. Add the eggplant slices—

don't crowd the pan—and fry until golden on both sides. Set aside. Add the onions to the skillet and fry until they, too, are golden. Stir in the garlic, tomato, tomato paste and parsley. Add the water. Simmer until all the water has boiled away and the vegetables are soft. Take off the heat and mix in the meat. Season to taste with salt, freshly ground pepper and cinnamon.

Place a layer of the eggplant in the bottom of a buttered baking dish that can go to the table. Top with the meat mixture and finish with the remaining eggplant.

Add egg yolks to Béchamel one at a time, beating hard after each addition. Pour sauce over the eggplant. Bake about 45 minutes, or until the eggplant tests tender when pierced with a fork and there is a nice brown crust on top.

Cool for about 15 minutes, then serve to 4 or 5 straight from the baking dish, along with a big green salad.

LAMB STUFFED EGGPLANTS

These can be served as a first course at dinner, although they are rather sturdy, but they make a splendid main dish for lunch.

4 medium eggplants

3 tablespoons butter or margarine

2 tablespoons vegetable oil

1 large yellow onion, peeled and chopped fine

2 cloves garlic, crushed, peeled and minced

½ cup cold water

1 cup cooked rice

1½ to 2 CUPS FINELY GROUND LEFTOVER LAMB

6 to 8 parsley sprigs, minced

½ cup walnuts, chopped (optional)

2 tablespoons tomato paste or catsup

Salt

Freshly ground black pepper

2 eggs, well beaten

Olive oil

Fine dry bread crumbs

Preheat oven to 350°.

Cut the eggplants in half and remove the pulp with a sharp knife, leaving a thin layer inside each shell. Chop the pulp fine and set aside.

Heat the butter and oil in a heavy skillet. Add the onion, garlic and the cold water. Cook until all the water has boiled away and the onion is soft and transparent. Add the eggplant pulp and sauté for about 4 minutes. Stir in all remaining ingredients except the eggs, olive oil and crumbs. Then stir in the eggs and cook, stirring, for about 2 minutes. Taste for seasoning.

Fill the eggplant shells with the mixture, spooning a little olive oil over each and then sprinkle with crumbs. Arrange in a baking pan or dish about 2 inches deep. Add about ½ inch of water and a few spoonfuls of oil.

Bake for about 40 minutes, basting occasionally with oil.

CURRIED LAMB

This recipe can also be used for chicken. In that case, replace the meat broth with chicken broth. If you have only 2 cups of meat make only half the sauce.

4 tablespoons (½ stick) butter	4 cups meat broth, heated
4 large onions, peeled and chopped fine	1 cup heavy cream
	Salt
2 large firm apples, cored and chopped fine	Freshly ground pepper
	Lemon juice, strained, to taste
1½ cups cold water	
2 to 3 tablespoons good curry powder	4 CUPS LEFTOVER LAMB
	Cooked rice
½ cup all-purpose flour	Condiments

Melt the butter in a large heavy saucepan. Add the onions, apples and cold water. Bring to a boil, reduce heat and cook over moderate heat until all the water has boiled away and both onions and apples are soft. If necessary add more water. Stir in the curry powder and flour until smooth. Cook, stirring constantly, for 3 to 4 minutes or until the mixture froths. Stir in the hot broth. Simmer for about 15 minutes, giving the mixture an occasional stir. Then stir in the cream, adding salt, pepper and lemon juice to taste. Finally, add the lamb and bring up to a boil. Do *not* cook further.

Serve to 6 with hot cooked rice, chutney (traditional with curry), cold beer (not wine) and five or six of the condiments listed below. Look into your refrigerator and your cupboards to see what you've got on hand that should be, or could be, used up.

Flaked coconut	Melon cubes
Crisp bacon pieces	Chopped fresh sweet peppers
Peanuts	Cherry tomatoes
Chopped cashew nuts	Sliced radishes
Chopped chives	Hard-cooked eggs, sliced
Chopped scallions	Raw or fried onion rings
Raisins soaked in brandy	Finely chopped celery
Fresh orange sections	Fresh pineapple wedges
Seedless grapes	Mushrooms Vinaigrette

Veal

Veal, Most Elegant Meat

If you are lucky enough to have a bit of cold roasted or braised veal on hand and want to turn it to good account you'll find here a handful of recipes. I have limited the recipes for the rather obvious reason that veal is currently a luxury that few of us can enjoy often. Therefore, no leftovers.

PSEUDO VITELLO TONNATO

Vitello Tonnato is a glorious summer dish bestowed on us by the Italians, and what I'm giving you here is not, in any sense, the equivalent of the real thing. But if you have enough leftover cooked veal (roasted or braised) you can improvise a quite delicious dish by using this sauce.

1 tablespoon onion juice
2 anchovy fillets, drained
  and chopped fine
1 3-ounce can of tuna in oil
1 cup mayonnaise

2 tablespoons capers, well
  drained and chopped
8 to 10 SLICES LEFTOVER VEAL
Cold parsleyed rice
Ripe tomatoes

Place the onion juice, anchovy fillets and tuna with the oil in an electric blender or food processor, blend until you have a smooth purée. Mix with the mayonnaise and the capers. Arrange cold veal on a platter and mask with the sauce.

Serve, with cold parsleyed rice and sliced ripe tomatoes, to 4 or 5.

BAKED VEAL BALLS

2 CUPS GROUND LEFTOVER VEAL
2 eggs, well beaten
Salt
Freshly ground pepper
Paprika

¼ teaspoon freshly grated
   nutmeg
¼ cup blanched almonds,
   chopped fine
1½ cups Tomato Sauce
   (page 233)

Preheat oven to 375°.

Work veal, eggs, seasonings and almonds together well.
Shape into small balls. Place in a casserole, cover with Tomato
Sauce and bake for about 30 minutes or until hot and bubbling.
Serves about 4.

VEAL TIMBALES

1 cup bread crumbs
1 cup milk or broth
2 CUPS GROUND LEFTOVER VEAL
2 eggs, well beaten
1 tablespoon grated onion

8 to 10 sprigs parsley, minced
½ teaspoon thyme
Salt
Freshly ground pepper
Butter or margarine

Preheat oven to 375°.

Combine crumbs and milk, then stir in the veal, eggs,
onion, parsley, thyme, salt and pepper to taste. Butter individual
molds (custard cups or ramekins), fill with the mixture and
place in a baking pan. Add enough hot water from the tap to
reach to two-thirds the depth of the molds. Bake for 30 to
40 minutes or until firm. Serves 4.

JELLIED VEAL LOAF

Vegetable oil
1 onion, peeled and grated
1 rib celery, minced
1½ cups chicken broth
  (page 59)
1 envelope unflavored
  gelatine
Juice of ½ lemon, strained
Salt
Freshly ground pepper
2 CUPS CHOPPED LEFTOVER
  VEAL

3 or 4 sprigs parsley, minced
1 tablespoon sweet green
  pepper, finely chopped
¼ cup well-drained pimientos,
  finely chopped
Garnish:
  Watercress
  3 hard-cooked eggs,
    quartered
  Dill pickles
  Black olives
  Radish roses

Brush a 2½-cup loaf mold with vegetable oil. Turn upside down on paper toweling to allow any excess to drain off.

Combine the onion, celery and 1 cup of the broth in a heavy saucepan. Bring to a boil and boil for 3 to 4 minutes. Push through a food mill or purée in an electric food processor. Pour back into the saucepan.

Meanwhile sprinkle the gelatine over the remaining ½ cup cold broth to soften. Add to hot purée, place over moderate heat and stir until the gelatine has dissolved. Add the lemon juice and season with salt and pepper. Refrigerate until the mixture mounds on a spoon. Then stir in all remaining ingredients, except the garnish. Salt and pepper to taste. Mix well. Spoon into the prepared mold, seal with plastic wrap and refrigerate until firm.

To serve, turn out onto a platter. Garnish with the watercress, eggs, pickles, olives and radishes.

A green salad, dressed with Sauce Vinaigrette (page 229), turns this into a pleasant hot-weather lunch. Should serve 4.

Pork

COLD ROAST PORK WITH HONEYDEW MELON

This makes a good main course for lunch.

8 SLICES LEFTOVER ROAST PORK,   *Black olives*
  AT ROOM TEMPERATURE   *Lemon wedges*
8 *slices ripe honeydew melon,*
  chilled

Trim all fat off the meat. Arrange alternate slices of meat and melon, overlapping, down the center of a chilled platter. Garnish with the olives and lemon.

Serve with salt and freshly ground black pepper.

ENGLISH PORK

Let's say you have leftover pork. You can turn it into an interesting dish with very little effort.

2 *tablespoons butter or*   1 *tablespoon all-purpose flour*
  margarine   *Salt*
4 GENEROUS SLICES LEFTOVER   *Freshly ground pepper*
  PORK   ¾ *cup gravy or Brown Sauce*
1 *medium yellow onion,*   *(page 11)*
  peeled and coarsely   1 *teaspoon vinegar*
  chopped   1 *teaspoon mustard*

Melt the butter in a heavy skillet. Add the pork and brown lightly on both sides. Lift from the pan to a heated serving platter and keep warm. Add the onion to the skillet and sauté until a good brown color. Sprinkle with flour. Add salt and pepper to taste. Stir well and cook, stirring occasionally, until the flour has browned. Stir in the gravy, vinegar and mustard. Bring up to a boil, then pour over the meat. Serves 4.

PORK TETRAZZINI

4 tablespoons (½ stick) butter
   or margarine
1 8-ounce package noodles
5 or 6 fresh button
   mushrooms, sliced
1 medium yellow onion,
   peeled and chopped fine
3 tablespoons all-purpose flour
1½ cups milk

1 cup dry white jug wine
2 teaspoons salt
Several twists of the
   peppermill
Dash cayenne pepper
2 CUPS CUBED LEFTOVER PORK
2 tablespoons freshly grated
   Parmesan cheese

Preheat oven to 400°.

Butter a 1½-quart soufflé or baking dish. Set aside.

Cook the noodles according to package directions *al dente* (firm to the bite). Drain.

Heat the remaining butter in a heavy skillet. Add the mushrooms and onion and cook, stirring often, until the onion is soft and transparent. Do not brown. Stir in the flour until smooth. Cook until it froths, about 3 or 4 minutes. Add milk and wine gradually, whipping constantly with a wire whip. Continue to cook, until the sauce comes to a boil. Season with salt, pepper and cayenne to taste. Finally, add the pork. Bring up to a boil slowly, giving it an occasional stir. Do not cook further.

Lift cooked noodles to a baking dish. Then coat with the meat sauce and sprinkle with the cheese. Bake for about 15 minutes or until the top is golden and the dish piping hot. Serves 6.

PORK STEW, SOUTHERN STYLE

2 tablespoons bacon fat

3 CUPS LEFTOVER PORK, CUT
  INTO 1-INCH CUBES

2 cups meat broth (page 10)

Dash cayenne pepper

Dash mace

1/2 teaspoon sage

1/2 teaspoon thyme

8 to 10 small white onions,
  cooked

1 1/2 tablespoons quick-cooking
  tapioca

Salt

Freshly ground pepper

Heat the bacon fat in a heavy saucepan. Add the pork and brown lightly. Stir in the broth and all the seasonings. Bring to a high boil. Add the onions and the tapioca. Bring to a high boil again, stirring constantly. Season to taste with salt and pepper.

Serve with hot biscuits and a green salad to 4.

CURRIED PORK AND
MACARONI SALAD

1 1/2 tablespoons vegetable,
  peanut or olive oil

1 tablespoon white wine
  vinegar

1 tablespoon minced chives

1/2 teaspoon dry mustard

1/2 teaspoon salt

Several twists of the
  peppermill

1 1/2 CUPS SLIVERED LEFTOVER
  PORK

1 medium cucumber, peeled,
  seeded and diced

2 teaspoons vegetable oil

1/2 teaspoon curry powder

1/2 cup mayonnaise

2 cups cooked elbow macaroni

Chicory, shredded

Sliced radishes

Mix oil, vinegar, chives and mustard with salt and pepper. Add the pork and toss well. Marinate at room temperature for 1 full hour or better, tossing several times.

Place the cucumbers in a colander, sprinkle with salt and allow to drain for 30 minutes. Meanwhile, heat the vegetable oil and stir in the curry powder until smooth. Cool and mix with the mayonnaise.

To finish the salad, combine the pork, cucumbers, mayonnaise and macaroni, mixing well with your hands.

Line a big salad bowl with the shredded chicory. Place the salad mixture on top and garnish with sliced radishes. My guess is it will make a good meal for 4 or 5.

PORK CROQUETTES

1 tablespoon butter or
    margarine
2 green onion bulbs, minced,
    or 1/4 small onion,
    peeled and minced
2 tablespoons all-purpose flour
1/2 cup meat broth (page 10)
2 CUPS FINELY GROUND LEAN
    LEFTOVER PORK

1/4 teaspoon sage
Pinch marjoram
Salt
Freshly ground pepper
1 egg, lightly beaten
Bread crumbs
Fat for deep frying

Melt the butter in a heavy skillet. Add onion and fry until lightly browned. Stir in the flour and cook, stirring, until the mixture froths, 2 to 3 minutes. Beat in the broth. Bring to a boil, reduce heat, and simmer for 5 to 6 minutes. Add the pork, sage and marjoram. Season well with salt and pepper. Stir over the heat until well mixed. Turn out on a plate and cool. Once cool, shape into small "corks" or cylinders, dip each croquette into the egg, then coat with crumbs. Dry on a wire rack for about 1 hour.

To fry, heat the fat to 375° on a candy thermometer or until a cube of bread browns in 60 seconds. Fry from 2 to 4 minutes or until golden. Do not fry too many at one time. Drain on paper towels. Serves 4 or 5. Good with applesauce.

Croquettes can be held briefly in a warm (200° oven) or they can be frozen (be sure to freezer-wrap). To reheat, place on a baking sheet in a preheated 400° oven for 15 to 20 minutes.

PORK PIE

This pie really needs gravy. You can make it by using the bones and trimmings from the roast or you can use Brown Sauce (page 11) diluted with stock to the right consistency.

Butter or margarine	*1 tablespoon onion juice**
Brown bread crumbs	*Salt*
2 CUPS FINELY CHOPPED LEAN LEFTOVER PORK	*Freshly ground pepper*
	*¾ cup milk***
2 cups mashed potatoes	*1 cup gravy*

Preheat oven to 350°.

Coat a pie pan with butter, then coat well with bread crumbs. Dump out any excess. Set aside.

Combine pork, potatoes and onion juice. Season highly with salt and pepper. Then work in enough milk to bind the mixture together. Place the mixture in the prepared pie pan, smooth the surface, and bake for 45 minutes. Serves 4.

---

* Cut an onion in half and squeeze on a reamer just the way you do an orange.
** Use soured cream or milk if you have some you would like to get rid of.

Ham

SLICED HAM WITH SAUCE PIQUANTE À LA CRÈME

This recipe makes about 2 cups of sauce. The number of servings will depend on how much meat you have left over.

4 green onion bulbs, peeled and chopped very fine

2 or 3 juniper berries, crushed

6 tablespoons wine vinegar

4 tablespoons butter or margarine

2 tablespoons all-purpose flour

1 cup meat broth (page 10), heated

6 tablespoons dry white jug wine

Salt

Freshly ground pepper

½ cup heavy cream, heated

Cold leftover ham, thinly sliced

Preheat oven to 300°.

Combine the green onions, juniper berries and vinegar in a small saucepan. Bring to a boil and cook until all the vinegar has boiled away.

In a second pan, melt half the butter, stir in flour and cook over moderate heat stirring constantly until the mixture is perfectly smooth and turns a pale coffee color. Add the hot broth, beating constantly with a wire whip. Continue to cook, beating, until the sauce thickens. Add the wine and onion mixture. Cook slowly for about 30 minutes, giving mixture an occasional stir. Skim off any scum that rises to the surface. Strain into a clean saucepan, bring to a boil again, season with salt and pepper, then stir in the hot cream. Finish with the remaining butter.

Arrange slices of ham in a big shallow baking dish. Pour the hot sauce over them and heat slowly in the oven, 10 to 15 minutes.

HAM AND CHEESE SOUFFLÉ

3 tablespoons butter
1 cup grated Swiss cheese
  (about 1/4 pound)
3 tablespoons all-purpose flour
1 cup milk
Salt
Pinch cayenne pepper

Pinch grated nutmeg
4 eggs, separated
1/2 CUP FINELY DICED LEFTOVER
  HAM
2 extra egg whites
Cream of tartar

Preheat oven to 375°.

Butter a 1½-quart soufflé dish well, including the curve at the bottom. Coat with cheese, dumping any excess back into the cup. Refrigerate.

Melt the remaining butter in a heavy saucepan. Stir in the flour and cook, stirring constantly, over low heat until the mixture froths, 2 to 3 minutes. Add the milk and cook, beating with a wire whip, until the sauce thickens. Stir in the seasonings. Add the egg yolks one at a time, beating hard after each addition. Finally, stir in the cheese and ham.

Beat the egg whites with a pinch of salt and cream of tartar until they hold firm, shiny peaks when the beater is held straight up. Pour the ham mixture over the whites and fold in with a rubber spatula. Pour into the prepared dish and place on a baking sheet. Bake for about 30 minutes. Serve at once.

HAM AND ASPARAGUS
HOLLANDAISE

Plan on 4 spears of asparagus and 2 slices of leftover ham for
each person.

Freshly cooked very thin   VERY THIN SLICES COOKED HAM
   asparagus   *Hollandaise Sauce (page 146)*

Cut off the tough ends of the asparagus, peel from the top
down, then cook, uncovered, in boiling salted water 3 to 4
minutes or until the stem ends can be pierced with a sharp
knife. Lift to a napkin and keep warm.

    To serve, roll up 2 spears in a slice of the ham. Arrange,
seam side down, on a heated serving platter and coat with
Hollandaise Sauce.

HAM MOUSSE

Vegetable oil   *⅛ teaspoon cream of tartar*
3 envelopes unflavored   *Salt*
   gelatine   *Freshly ground white pepper*
2 cups Sauce Velouté (page   *3 egg whites*
   231)*   *1 cup heavy cream, whipped*
2 CUPS DICED LEFTOVER HAM
  (OR THE SAME AMOUNT OF
  CHICKEN OR DUCK)

Line the bottom of a 6-cup mold with kitchen parchment
and brush *the sides only* with vegetable oil. Turn upside down
to drain on paper towels. Set aside.

---

* Make the Sauce Velouté in these proportions: 3 tablespoons butter or
margarine; 3 tablespoons flour; 2 cups poultry broth; salt and freshly
ground pepper to taste.

Sprinkle the gelatine over the hot Sauce Velouté. Place back over a low heat for 2 minutes, stirring constantly, to dissolve the gelatine. Take off the heat and add the ham.

Purée half the ham and sauce in a blender at high speed or in an electric food processor. Then purée the remainder. Return to the saucepan and keep warm over very low heat.

Sprinkle the cream of tartar and a good pinch of salt and pepper over the egg whites and beat with a rotary or electric beater (or in an electric mixer) until the whites hold firm, shiny peaks when the beater is held straight up. Pour the ham mixture over the whites and fold in with a rubber spatula. Refrigerate, giving mixture an occasional stir, until *almost cool and beginning to set.*

Fold the whipped cream into the cooled ham mixture, then spoon into the prepared mold. Refrigerate until firm. It will take at least 3 hours.

To serve, unmold on a chilled serving platter and garnish with leaves of Bibb lettuce or bouquets of watercress. Serve with toast points to about 10.

HAM AND EGG CASSEROLE

2 tablespoons butter
1 cup medium Sauce
  Béchamel (page 230)
¼ cup chili sauce

1 CUP DICED LEFTOVER HAM
4 hard-cooked eggs, sliced
¼ cup bread crumbs

Preheat oven to 375°.

Butter a 1-quart baking dish thoroughly. Combine Sauce Béchamel and chili sauce. Layer ham and eggs in the prepared casserole, coating each layer with some of the sauce. Finish the dish with bread crumbs and dot with the remaining butter. Bake until piping hot and the crumbs have browned lightly, about 25 minutes. Serves 5 or 6.

HAM AND POTATO CROQUETTES

3 Idaho potatoes
½ CUP MINCED LEFTOVER HAM
1 egg
Salt
Freshly ground white pepper

Freshly grated nutmeg
3 tablespoons vegetable oil
3 tablespoons butter or
  margarine

Peel the potatoes and grate very fine. Place in a bowl along with the ham and egg, and season with salt, pepper and nutmeg. Mix very well. Using 2 spoons, shape into small croquettes.

Heat the oil and butter in a heavy skillet. Sauté the croquettes in the hot fat until golden on both sides. As they finish cooking, place on a hot serving platter and keep warm. Makes 12 to 15 croquettes.

LIMA BEAN AND HAM LOAF

6 tablespoons (¾ stick) butter
  or margarine
1 cup cooked lima beans
¼ cup chili sauce or catsup
½ CUP MINCED LEFTOVER HAM
2 eggs, lightly beaten

1 yellow onion, peeled and
  minced
1 cup soft bread crumbs
  page (197)
Salt
Freshly ground pepper
Tomato Sauce (page 233)

Preheat oven to 350°.

Butter a shallow baking pan. Set aside.

Combine beans and 2 tablespoons of the butter, melted, with the chili sauce in the container of an electric blender. Blend at high speed until you have a smooth purée.

Mix together with all remaining ingredients, except the butter. Season with salt and pepper to taste. Best done with your hands.

Place in the prepared baking pan and shape into a loaf. Dot with remaining butter and bake for 30 minutes. Serve with Tomato Sauce (page 233) to 4 or 5.

HAM RAMEKINS

Butter or margarine
2 eggs, separated
¾ CUP FINELY CHOPPED
    LEFTOVER HAM
4 tablespoons milk
½ teaspoon Spice Parisienne*

½ scant teaspoon prepared
    mustard
Salt
Freshly ground pepper
Cream of tartar
Cayenne pepper

Preheat oven to 350°.

Butter 8 ramekins well, including the curve at the bottom. Set aside.

Beat the egg yolks lightly, then combine with the ham, milk, Spice Parisienne, mustard, salt and pepper to taste. Fill the ramekins about three-fourths full of the mixture. Bake until the mixture is set.

Meanwhile, sprinkle the egg whites with a little salt and a pinch of cream of tartar. Then beat until they hold firm, shiny peaks when the beater is held straight up. Mound on top of the ham mixture in the ramekins, dividing it evenly. Sprinkle very lightly with cayenne, return to the oven and bake until the meringue is golden. Serve piping hot.

* Spice Parisienne, called *quatre épices* in France, is usually a mixture of pepper, nutmeg, ground cloves and cinnamon or ginger.

RED BEANS AND T'INGS

This hearty dish comes from Trinidad and as you have probably guessed "t'ings" translates into "things."

½ pound dry red beans or　　4 *cups cooked rice*
　　kidney beans　　　　　　¾ CUP COARSELY CHOPPED
Salt　　　　　　　　　　　　LEFTOVER HAM
Freshly ground pepper　　2 *or* 3 *whole green onions,*
1 *bay leaf*　　　　　　　　　　*chopped*

Pick over and wash the beans. Place in a heavy kettle and
add cold water to cover. Cover and bring up to a boil over
high heat. Take off the heat and allow to soak for 1 hour.
Add salt and pepper to taste and the bay leaf. Place back
over medium heat and cook until tender, adding more water if
necessary. Drain thoroughly. Pour into a large heavy skillet,
stir in the rice, ham and onion. Taste for seasoning. Stir over
a good heat until piping hot. Serves 4.

HAM SOUP WITH PARMESAN

¾ CUP CHOPPED LEFTOVER　　1 *yellow onion, peeled and*
　　HAM　　　　　　　　　　　*minced*
4 *cups poultry broth (page* 59)　2 *egg yolks*
3 *tablespoons butter or*　　6 *to* 8 *slices oven-dried bread*
　　margarine　　　　　　　　½ *cup grated Parmesan*
　　　　　　　　　　　　　　　　cheese (about 2 *ounces)*

Combine the ham with a cup or so of the chicken broth in
the container of an electric blender. Blend at high speed to
make a smooth purée. Pour into a saucepan.

　　Melt the butter in another saucepan, add the onion and
cook, stirring frequently, until golden. Spoon into blender or
an electric food processor with some of the broth and blend

at high speed. Combine with the ham mixture and any broth remaining in the saucepan. Bring to a boil and simmer for about 30 minutes.

Beat the yolks lightly in a heated soup tureen. Add the hot soup gradually, beating constantly with a wire whip.

To serve, place a piece of the oven-dried bread in each heated soup plate and add a ladle or two of the soup. Sprinkle with Parmesan. Serve to 5 or 6.

COLD HAM LOAF

2 envelopes unflavored
    gelatine
1½ cups poultry broth
    (page 59), heated
2 CUPS GROUND LEFTOVER HAM
2 teaspoons prepared
    horseradish
1 pimiento, minced
Juice of ½ yellow onion

1 teaspoon Worcestershire
    sauce
Juice of ½ lemon, strained
¼ teaspoon freshly grated
    nutmeg
½ teaspoon mace
½ cup mayonnaise
Whipped Cream and
    Horseradish Sauce
    (page 234)

Sprinkle the gelatine over the chicken broth and stir over low heat until dissolved. Refrigerate until it begins to thicken and will mound on a spoon, then mix in remaining ingredients (except sauce) in the order listed. Pour into a 5- to 6-cup mold and refrigerate until firm.

To unmold, run a small spatula around the edge, then dip the mold into hot water. Invert on a serving platter. Serve with Whipped Cream and Horseradish Sauce. Serves 4 to 5.

CRÊPES WITH HAM

This is a marvelous way to use the last scraps of ham on the bone.

Make some crêpes (page 204).

Filling:

3 tablespoons butter	*Salt*
2 level tablespoons all-purpose flour	*Freshly ground pepper*
1 cup milk	*1 egg yolk*
	1 CUP MINCED LEFTOVER HAM

Preheat oven to 400°.

Melt 2 tablespoons of butter in a heavy saucepan. Stir in the flour and cook, stirring constantly, until the mixture froths. Add the milk. Cook, beating constantly with a wire whip, until the mixture begins to thicken. Season with salt and pepper to taste. Beat in the egg yolk vigorously. Stir in the minced ham. Set the mixture aside to cool. When cold it should be very thick.

To finish, lay each crêpe separately on your work surface. Place 2 tablespoons of the ham mixture on each one. Fold the crêpe over the filling, then roll it up.

Place finished crêpes in a baking dish and place in a hot oven for 10 or 15 minutes until warmed. Serves 6 to 8.

BLACK BEAN SOUP

½ pound dry black beans
Water
1 MEATY HAM BONE
6 cups chicken broth
2 green peppers, seeded, ribs
    removed, and diced
3 large yellow onions, peeled
    and chopped fine

2 cloves garlic, crushed, peeled
    and minced
2 bay leaves
¼ pound salt pork, diced
2 tablespoons dry sherry
2 cups cooked white rice,
    heated
Olive oil
White wine vinegar

Wash the beans, place in a bowl and cover with water. Soak overnight. Pour the beans and their soaking liquid into a large, heavy kettle. Add the ham bone, broth, peppers, ⅓ of the chopped onion, half the garlic and both bay leaves. Bring to a boil, reduce heat to simmer, cover, and cook until the beans are tender, about 3 hours.

Meanwhile, brown the salt pork in a skillet over fairly high heat. Add half the remaining onions and all the remaining garlic. Add a cup of water. Bring to a boil and cook over moderate heat until all the water has boiled away and the onions are tender.

Lift the bone from the kettle. Cut off any meat and toss into the soup. Discard the bone. Stir the onions into the soup along with the sherry. Skim the fat from the soup.

To serve, place a serving of the rice in a heated soup plate and add a ladle or two of soup. Pass around the remaining raw onion, with a cruet of olive oil and another of vinegar, as a condiment. Serves about 8.

SPLIT PEA SOUP

This soup freezes perfectly. We suggest 1-quart jars, leaving enough space at the top for expansion. Add cream, in same proportions (see below), after thawing.

HAM BONE

4 cups (two 1-pound boxes)
quick-cooking split peas

2 yellow onions, peeled, each
stuck with 2 cloves

2 bay leaves

6 to 8 peppercorns

3 ribs celery with tops,
coarsely chopped

3 large carrots, washed,
coarsely chopped

5 to 6 quarts cold water

2 tablespoons tomato paste

Heavy cream or milk

Minced parsley

Place all ingredients except the tomato paste, cream and parsley in a large kettle. Add enough cold water to cover and bring up to a boil. Reduce heat, then simmer, covered, until the peas are very soft. This will take several hours. Lift the bone out of the kettle and set aside.

Push the soup and the vegetables through a fine sieve or food mill, or purée in an electric food processor. Then stir the tomato paste into the thick purée. In the event there is any meat on the bone, cut it off, sliver it and set aside to use as a garnish. Discard the bone.

To serve, dilute the purée with heavy cream (allow a cup or so of cream to 4 cups of purée). Taste for seasoning. You may find you need both salt and pepper.

Serve the soup in large heated soup plates with a garnish of the slivered ham (if any) and minced parsley. Makes about 8 servings.

WHITE BEAN AND NOODLE SOUP

2 cups (1 pound) dry white
  beans
½ pound fresh pork skin
  (optional)
1 HAM BONE
1 onion, peeled and chopped
  fine
1 carrot, peeled and chopped
  fine

1 rib celery, chopped fine
4 tablespoons oil
1 tablespoon salt
Cold water to cover
½ pound ribbon noodles or
  spaghetti
Freshly ground pepper
Grated Parmesan cheese

Soak the beans overnight or use the following quick method. Bring measured amount of water to boiling point (allow about 3 quarts of water to 1 pound of beans). Add the washed beans, bring to a boil again and boil exactly 2 minutes. Take off the heat, cover and allow to stand for one hour.

Chop the pork skin into pieces. Combine beans, pork skin, ham bone, onion, carrot, celery, and 2 tablespoons of the oil in a large heavy casserole. Add salt and enough cold water to cover. Bring to a boil, reduce heat, cover and simmer for 2½ hours. Discard the ham bone.

Take about half the beans from the pan with a cup or so of the liquid. Purée in an electric blender or in an electric food processor. Return to the casserole and bring the soup up to a boil. Add the noodles and cook over a good heat until *al dente* (firm to the bite). Sprinkle with salt and freshly ground pepper to taste.

Finally, stir in the remaining oil. Pour into soup bowls and cool to lukewarm. *This soup is never served hot.* Sprinkle lightly with Parmesan cheese before serving. Serves 6.

Scraps of Cooked Ham Turned to Good Account

Add chopped and shredded ham to any tomato or cheese sauce served with spaghetti or rice.

Add chopped ham to seasoned spaghetti or rice before serving.

Add chopped or shredded ham to omelets either before cooking or before folding.

Add coarsely chopped ham to green salads before dressing.

Add chopped ham to hot salad dressing for cabbage, fresh spinach or potato salad.

Add chopped ham to scalloped or creamed potatoes.

Place a layer of minced ham between two wafer-thin baking powder biscuits before baking. Serve hot as appetizers.

Mix about 2 cups finely ground ham with 4 tablespoons finely chopped sweet or sour pickles, a pinch each of ginger, ground cloves and nutmeg, and enough mayonnaise to make a spreadable paste.

Six Ways to Devil Cooked Ham for Sandwiches

To 2 cups ground ham add any of the following:

1. ⅓ cup chopped sweet pickle with enough mayonnaise to bind the mixture together.

2. ½ cup finely chopped chutney.

3. 2 teaspoons prepared mustard and enough mayonnaise to make the mixture spreadable.

4. ½ cup coarsely chopped peanuts with just enough mayonnaise to hold the mixture together.

5. ½ cup chopped dill pickles with sufficient mayonnaise to bind the mixture.

6. 2 tablespoons catsup and ¼ teaspoon of Tabasco.

Bacon

Bacon Bits with Vegetables

Bacon and/or its drippings does marvelous things for most green vegetables.

Shredded cabbage can be stir-fried in bacon fat.

Cooked green beans, drained and dried, are delicious tossed in the frying pan with bits of bacon and slivered green onions.

Add fried bits of bacon, vinegar and a soupçon of sugar to cooked greens such as spinach or lettuce. A splendid companion to poultry or chops.

Bacon Rind

When recipes using bacon say, "Cut off the rind," cut it off by all means, but wash it and save to flavor soup and vegetables.

POULTRY

Storing Poultry

Fresh poultry stored in the refrigerator should have the giblets removed (wrapped and refrigerated separately) and the poultry itself should be wrapped and placed in the coldest part of the refrigerator. Poultry stored in the freezer should be freezer wrapped, sealed, labeled and dated. THE FREEZER MUST MAINTAIN ZERO TEMPERATURE. I recommend that you keep thermometers in both your refrigerator and freezer.

The following chart giving recommended *maximum* storage time for fresh and frozen poultry comes from the U.S. Department of Agriculture and the National Broiler Council.

STORAGE TIME CHART FOR POULTRY

FRESH POULTRY	REFRIGERATOR 35° to 40° F.	FREEZER 0° F.
Whole chicken and turkey	1 to 2 days	12 months
Chicken and turkey pieces	1 to 2 days	6 months
Whole ducks and geese	1 to 2 days	6 months
Giblets	1 to 2 days	3 months
COOKED POULTRY		
Pieces covered with broth	1 to 2 days	2 months
Pieces, *not covered*	1 to 2 days	1 month
Cooked poultry dishes	1 to 2 days	2 months

FRESH POULTRY	REFRIGERATOR 35° to 40° F.	FREEZER 0° F.
Fried chicken	1 to 2 days	2 months
Commercially frozen chicken		12 months
Home-frozen chicken	2 days	4 to 6 months
Thawed chicken, any kind	Use immediately. *Do not refreeze.*	

Poultry Sandwiches and Salads

CHICKEN SANDWICHES

As everybody knows, or should, leftover chicken and turkey make wonderful sandwiches. Undoubtedly, the Club Sandwich, an American original, is the best known. Correctly (and I use this word advisedly), it is made like this: freshly made crisp buttered toast, a lettuce leaf, a dollop of mayonnaise, slices of chicken or turkey breast, sliced ripe tomato, a bit of salt, crisp bacon, more mayonnaise and the remaining piece of toast. Green olives and sweet pickles are the correct garnishes.

CHICKEN SALAD

Chicken or turkey salad (both light and dark meat, cut in big, generous pieces) is made with mayonnaise (preferably home-made, page 139), seasoned well with salt and freshly ground pepper, served in a bowl with a garland of lettuce leaves and a garnish of capers, well-drained. Extra mayonnaise is served on the side. A handful of fresh seedless grapes is sometimes added, or a few coarsely chopped walnuts. The mayonnaise can be varied by adding a bit of sour cream—2 to 3 tablespoons per cup of mayonnaise.

Poultry Bones and Broth

POULTRY BROTH

CARCASS OF A CHICKEN, HEN
   OR CAPON, OR OF TURKEY,
   GOOSE OR DUCK
NECK, GIZZARD AND HEART*
3 to 4 sprigs parsley
1 bay leaf
Good pinch thyme

1 onion stuck with 2 cloves
1 rib celery, coarsely chopped
1 carrot, washed and coarsely
   chopped
1 tablespoon salt
About 6 peppercorns
Cold water

Break up the carcass of the bird if necessary. Place in a large heavy saucepan or casserole. Add all the ingredients and enough cold water to cover. Bring to a boil slowly. Reduce heat to simmer, cover and cook for about 2 hours. Strain through a fine sieve. Pour into pint containers, cover securely and refrigerate immediately. Freeze if you are not going to use the broth within a few days. Makes 6 to 8 cups.

CONSOMMÉ AURORA

1½ tablespoons quick-cooking
   tapioca
¼ cup tomato purée
4 cups poultry broth

1 CUP JULIENNED LEFTOVER
CHICKEN WHITE MEAT OR
TURKEY
Salt
Freshly ground pepper

* Freeze the liver (page 57).

Combine the tapioca, tomato purée and broth in a heavy
saucepan. Cover and cook until the tapioca is transparent. Add
the chicken and bring to a boil. Taste for seasoning. Serves
4 to 5.

AVGOLEMONO SOUP
(*Egg and Lemon Soup*)

An elegant Greek soup with which to open an important dinner.

6 CUPS POULTRY BROTH	*1 teaspoon flour*
(PAGE 59)	*1/4 cup water*
Salt	*3 eggs*
1/2 cup rice, uncooked	*Juice 2 lemons, strained*

Pour broth in a large saucepan. Add salt and rice. Cover, bring
to a boil, reduce heat and simmer for 20 minutes. Strain 3 cups
of the broth (no rice) into a smaller saucepan. Cover the
remaining broth and rice and keep hot over very low heat.

Mix the flour with the water until smooth. Whip into the
3 cups of broth. Bring to a boil, then simmer for 5 minutes.
Break the eggs into a large bowl and beat with a rotary or electric
beater until very thick and pale yellow. Add the boiling stock
slowly, beating constantly. Then beat in the lemon juice. Now
pour this mixture into the rice and broth and mix thoroughly.
Do not cook further or the soup will curdle.

Serve at once in heated soup cups to 8.

RICH CHICKEN SOUP

4 cups poultry broth (page 59)
2 tablespoons grated onion
½ cup fine unseasoned
cracker crumbs
2½ cups milk
1 CUP FINELY GROUND
LEFTOVER CHICKEN, TURKEY
OR GOOSE

3 hard-cooked egg yolks, well
mashed
½ cup light cream
Salt
Freshly ground white pepper

Combine the broth and onion in a heavy saucepan and bring to a boil. Reduce heat and simmer 10 minutes. Meanwhile, soak the cracker crumbs in ½ cup of the milk for about 5 minutes. Mix the meat and yolks together, then combine with the crumb mixture. Stir in the remaining milk and the cream. Add to the hot broth. Season to taste with salt and pepper. Bring up to a boil but do not boil. Place over very low heat or on a Flame Tamer* for about an hour, being very careful to avoid curdling. The flavor seems to improve with this mellowing period. If you like a thicker soup add more cracker crumbs. Should serve about 8.

* A Flame Tamer, a thick metal cylinder made of durable metal with air vents (there are many variations), makes every pan a double boiler. Food can't scorch or burn; it prevents glass and earthenware casseroles from cracking. To use, just sit it right over the gas or electric burner.

LETTUCE SOUP WITH CHICKEN

2 heads Boston lettuce, well
   washed, or 1 large romaine
4 tablespoons (½ stick)
   butter or margarine
8 cups poultry broth (page 59)
1 CUP DICED LEFTOVER CHICKEN,
   TURKEY, DUCK OR GOOSE

1 cup heavy cream
2 egg yolks, slightly beaten
Freshly grated nutmeg
Salt
Freshly ground pepper
Minced parsley

Shred the lettuce very fine. Melt the butter in a heavy saucepan.
Add the lettuce and soften for 2 to 3 minutes. Add the broth,
cover and simmer for about 20 minutes. Purée with the diced
chicken, a small amount at a time, in an electric food processor
or blender. Rinse out the saucepan and return the purée. Reheat
the soup.

    Bring the cream to a boil. Add a little to the beaten yolks.
Combine the two, beating hard. Taste for seasoning. Add to
the soup. Bring up to a boil but do not boil. Spoon into heated
soup plates and garnish with parsley. Serves 8 to 10.

TURKEY CELERY BROTH

This is a nice simple broth that can be served alone, but it can
also be used successfully as a base for making other soups,
making sauces or cooking vegetables.

TURKEY, CHICKEN, DUCK OR
   GOOSE CARCASS, BROKEN UP
NECK AND GIZZARD
Leftover dressing, if any
Leftover gravy, if any
2 large yellow onions, cut in
   half, each stuck with 2
   cloves
1 large carrot, washed and
   coarsely chopped

1 bay leaf
4 or 5 sprigs parsley
About 8 peppercorns
1 teaspoon thyme
6 to 8 ribs celery, washed and
   sliced thin
Salt
Freshly ground pepper
Cold water to cover
   generously

Combine all ingredients in a large heavy kettle. Bring to a boil, reduce heat to simmer, cover and cook for 2 hours. Strain and discard the bones, etc. Taste here for salt and pepper.

After straining, pour into pint Mason jars and refrigerate or freeze (leave head space). Makes 6 to 7 cups.

TURKEY CHOWDER

TURKEY, CHICKEN, DUCK OR
   GOOSE CARCASS, BROKEN UP
Any scraps of leftover meat
Any leftover stuffing
Any leftover gravy
2 ribs celery, chopped
1 yellow onion, split, stuck
   with 2 cloves
1 or 2 carrots, coarsely
   chopped
A few peppercorns

1 bay leaf
1 teaspoon dried thyme
Cold water to cover, at least
   8 cups
1 large raw potato, peeled and
   diced
½ to 1 cup cooked vegetables
Cooked rice (at least ¾ cup)
Minced chives or parsley
Salt
Freshly ground pepper

Place all ingredients, except the potato, vegetables, rice, chives and seasonings, in a large kettle, and bring slowly to a boil. Reduce heat, cover, and simmer for about 2 hours. Strain. Discard bones and vegetables. Reduce over a high heat until you have about 6 cups left. Add the potato. Cook 10 minutes. Add vegetables just long enough to heat through. Taste for seasoning. You'll probably need both salt and pepper.

To serve, place a couple of tablespoons of rice in a heated soup bowl, add soup and sprinkle with the chives. Let's say it will serve 6.

OLD-FASHIONED GIBLET AND BARLEY SOUP

2 tablespoons fat
1 yellow onion, peeled and
* sliced thin*
5½ cups cold water
CHICKEN, TURKEY, GOOSE OR
  DUCK GIBLETS, NECK AND
  CARCASS (BROKEN UP)*
1 teaspoon salt

½ teaspoon celery salt
1 can (16-ounce size)
* tomatoes, cut up*
1 cup pearl barley
1 teaspoon beef stock base
½ teaspoon thyme
Any leftover meat, cut up

Place the fat, onion and ½ cup of the water in a large heavy kettle. Boil until all the water has evaporated and the onion sizzles. Add the giblets, neck, carcass, salt, celery salt and remaining 5 cups of water. Bring to a boil. Reduce heat, cover and simmer 1 hour. Lift out giblets, neck and carcass. Cut any meat off neck and carcass; chop giblets fine. Return the meat to kettle. Add any leftover meat. Then add all remaining ingredients. Bring up to a boil, cover, and simmer 1 hour longer. Makes about 2 quarts.

* Freeze the liver (page 57).

FRICASSEED BIRD WITH
POTATO DUMPLINGS

LEFTOVER CHICKEN, TURKEY,
   DUCK OR GOOSE CARCASS,
   WINGS, NECK AND GIBLETS
3 teaspoons salt
Several twists of the
   peppermill
1/4 teaspoon ginger
6 cups poultry broth (page 59)
1 yellow onion, peeled and
   sliced thin

2 ribs celery with tops (if any),
   chopped
1 clove garlic, peeled and
   crushed
4 tablespoons butter or fat
1/3 cup all-purpose flour
1 package (10-ounce size)
   frozen peas or carrots
Potato dumplings (see below)

Place all the ingredients except the fat, flour, frozen vegetables and dumplings in a large heavy kettle. Bring to a boil. Cover, reduce heat and simmer 2 hours, stirring occasionally. Strain into a bowl. Cut off any meat from carcass, wings, and neck (discard bones); cut up giblets and heart. Rinse out kettle. Add the butter and melt over moderate heat. Stir in flour and cook, stirring, until the mixture froths, 3 to 4 minutes. Add the strained broth, whipping constantly. Add the meat. Bring to a boil. Add the frozen vegetables and bring to a rolling boil again.

To serve, place 2 dumplings in a large heated soup plate and ladle fricassee over them. Serves 6.

Potato Dumplings

1 cup mashed potatoes
1 egg, lightly beaten
1/2 cup all-purpose flour

4 to 5 sprigs parsley, minced
Salt to taste
Dash freshly ground pepper

Combine all ingredients in a bowl and mix well. During the last 15 minutes of fricassee's simmering, drop the dumplings by tablespoons into the boiling mixture. When they rise to the surface, cover and simmer for 12 to 15 minutes. Makes 12.

Poultry Parts and Inmeats (Variety Meats)

CHICKEN WINGS WITH GINGER

When you've accumulated a nice little bag of frozen chicken wings, here's an interesting way to cook and serve them.

4 tablespoons soy sauce	8 LEFTOVER CHICKEN WINGS
¾ cup dry sherry	(ABOUT 1¼ POUNDS),
½ teaspoon ginger	THAWED
2 cloves garlic, crushed and	4 tablespoons all-purpose flour
peeled	Extra flour
	Fat for deep-fat frying

Combine the soy sauce, sherry, ginger and garlic in a plastic bag. Add the chicken wings. Squeeze out all air, mix well, and tie securely. Place in a pan in case of leakage and marinate for at least 4 hours or overnight, turning the bag occasionally. Strain the marinade into a bowl, and mix with the 4 tablespoons of flour until smooth. Coat the wings with the extra flour, then dip into the flour-marinade mixture. Place on a rack and allow to dry for about 1 hour.

To fry, heat the fat to 360° on a candy thermometer or until an inch cube of bread browns in one minute. Fry the wings, a few at a time, until crisp and golden—5 to 6 minutes. Serves 3 to 4.

CHOPPED CHICKEN AND LIVERS WITH MUSHROOMS

4 tablespoons (½ stick)
  butter or margarine
1 small yellow onion, peeled
  and sliced thin
3 cups (about ¼ pound)
  button mushrooms, sliced
½ POUND LEFTOVER CHICKEN
  LIVERS (ABOUT 6), THAWED
  AND CUT IN HALF

Salt
Freshly ground pepper
½ cup dry white wine
1 cup chopped leftover
  chicken
6 slices toasted white bread
Minced parsley

Melt the butter in a heavy skillet. Add the onion and mushrooms. Sauté, stirring frequently, until onions are golden. Stir in the chicken livers and cook 3 to 4 minutes. Season to taste with salt and pepper. Stir in the wine and the leftover chicken. Bring to a boil, then simmer for about 3 minutes. Taste for seasoning. Serve on toast with a sprinkling of parsley. Serves about 6.

ANITA'S FOIES DE POULETS EN FRICASSEE
(*Fricassee of Chicken Livers*)

6 tablespoons butter or
  margarine
1 cup diced cooked ham
2 POUNDS LEFTOVER CHICKEN
  LIVERS AND HEARTS, THAWED

12 fresh sage leaves or
  2 teaspoons dried
Salt
Freshly ground pepper
½ cup dry white jug wine

Melt 1 tablespoon of the butter in a skillet. Sauté the ham until golden. Set aside. Cut the chicken livers in two. Melt half the remaining butter with the sage leaves in the skillet. Cook very slowly for a few minutes to allow the butter to absorb the rich aroma of the sage. Add the hearts. Cook 5 minutes. Then add the livers and salt and pepper to taste. Cook over medium heat until firm. Stir in the ham. Cook 7 to 8 minutes, stirring constantly. The livers should be pink on the outside. Cooked too much they will be hard. Lift with a slotted spoon to a heated serving dish.

Add the white wine to the skillet and deglaze by boiling 2 to 3 minutes, scraping the bottom to loosen all the rich encrustations. Beat in the remaining butter, whipping constantly. Pour the sauce over the livers.

Serve with rice and freshly grated Parmesan cheese to 5 or 6.

CHICKEN LIVER SOUFFLÉ

4 tablespoons (½ stick)
  butter or margarine
Dry bread crumbs
6 LEFTOVER CHICKEN LIVERS,
  THAWED
2 cloves garlic, crushed, peeled
  and minced

1 cup thick Sauce Béchamel
  *(page 230)**
5 or 6 sprigs parsley, minced
4 whole eggs, separated
2 or 3 extra egg whites
Olive Sauce (page 233)

Preheat oven to 375°.

Butter a 1½-quart soufflé mold, including the curve at the bottom. Coat with bread crumbs. Dump out any excess and refrigerate.

Melt half the remaining butter in a skillet and sauté the livers with the garlic for about 5 minutes, taking care not to burn the garlic or it will taste bitter. Do not brown the livers. Chop the livers very fine and combine with the hot Sauce Béchamel and the parsley. With a wire whip, beat in the 4 egg

---

* Make the Sauce Béchamel in these proportions: 2 tablespoons butter or margarine; 2 tablespoons flour; 1 cup milk; salt and freshly ground pepper to taste.

yolks, one at a time, beating hard after each addition. The soufflé can be prepared to this point and set aside, sealed with plastic wrap.

Beat the egg whites until they hold firm, shiny peaks when the beater is held straight up. Whip about a third into the liver mixture vigorously with a wire whip. Pour over the remaining whites and fold in very gently with a rubber spatula.

Pour into the prepared mold, place on a baking sheet and bake for 30 to 35 minutes. Serve with Olive Sauce.

CHICKEN LIVER PÂTÉ

Always freeze the livers from chicken, ducks, turkeys or geese. When you have accumulated about 1 pound, turn them into a pâté. Here's how:

1 POUND LEFTOVER LIVERS
  (CHICKEN, DUCK, GOOSE
  AND/OR TURKEY), THAWED
Cold water to cover
1 *cup poultry broth (page 59)*
½ *cup (2 sticks) sweet butter*
  or margarine, melted

3 *green onion bulbs, minced*
Salt
Freshly ground pepper
Dash Cognac (optional)
1 *envelope unflavored*
  gelatine (optional)

Cut the livers in two. Place in a saucepan, cover with cold water and bring to a boil. Drain and wash under cold running water to get rid of the scum. Rinse out the saucepan and return the livers with the chicken broth. Bring to a boil, reduce heat, and simmer until very tender when pierced with the point of a paring knife. Drain through a fine sieve lined with two or three layers of dampened cheesecloth. Reserve the broth. Cut the livers coarsely and pureé, a few at a time, with some of the melted butter and the onions in the container of a blender or in an electric food processor. When all the livers are puréed, season with salt, pepper and Cognac, if you have a dollop on hand.

Take a 2-cup mold, cover the bottom with kitchen parchment. Spoon the pâté into the mold, smooth the surface and seal with plastic wrap. Refrigerate.

Garnish the serving dish with jelly. Here's how: Sprinkle an envelope of unflavored gelatine over the strained broth. Place over a low heat and stir until dissolved. Pour into a flat pan to a depth of about ¼ inch or a little better and refrigerate until firm. Cut into diamonds.

At serving time, turn the pâté out onto a platter that will hold it comfortably, remove and discard the parchment, and surround with the jelly diamonds.

GIBLET STEW

½ to 1 POUND LEFTOVER CHICKEN, TURKEY, DUCK OR GOOSE GIZZARDS, THAWED

½ to 1 POUND LEFTOVER CHICKEN, TURKEY, DUCK OR GOOSE HEARTS, THAWED

LEFTOVER CHICKEN, TURKEY, DUCK OR GOOSE PARTS: BACKS, NECKS, WING TIPS, THAWED*

1 big yellow onion, peeled, cut in half

1 or 2 carrots, washed and chopped

2 ribs celery with leaves, sliced

1 generous teaspoon dried thyme

6 or 8 peppercorns

2 quarts water

2 chicken bouillon cubes or 2 teaspoons instant chicken bouillon concentrate

Salt to taste

8 to 10 LEFTOVER CHICKEN, TURKEY, DUCK OR GOOSE LIVERS, THAWED

3 tablespoons butter or margarine

Grated rind of 1 lemon

Juice of 1 lemon, strained

½ cup dry white wine (optional)

2 cups hot cooked rice

Minced parsley

* Whenever you buy poultry, freeze the backs, necks and wing tips to use in making soups and always freeze the whole carcass, broken up, if you have roasted it whole. Add it, too, to soups. Freeze livers separately (page 57).

In a big soup kettle combine all ingredients down to and including bouillon. Bring to a boil, reduce heat to simmer, cover and cook for 1 hour and 15 minutes. Strain the soup, discarding bones and vegetables. Return the broth to the kettle. Taste here for salt. Place back over the heat and reduce over high heat to about 1½ quarts.

Slice the livers in half, cutting away any fat and connective tissues. Heat the butter in a heavy skillet. Add the livers and sauté until they have browned lightly but are still pink inside. Add the rind, lemon juice and wine. Keep warm but do not cook further.

Spoon the hot cooked rice into a heated vegetable dish. Scatter the livers on top and ladle all the pan juices over livers and rice. Sprinkle with parsley.

To serve, spoon rice and livers into large heated soup plates and ladle the hot broth over all. Serves about 6 deliciously.

GIBLET RICE

A refreshing accompaniment to a poached or roasted bird. Practical, too.

GIBLETS (EXCEPT THE LIVER), NECK AND WING TIPS FROM CHICKEN, TURKEY, DUCK OR GOOSE
1½ cups water
2 small yellow onions, peeled and chopped
Salt
Freshly ground pepper
1 bay leaf
2 tablespoons butter or margarine
1 cup long grain rice, uncooked
6 to 7 sprigs parsley, minced

Place the giblets, neck and wing tips in a heavy saucepan. Add 1½ cups of water, one of the onions, salt and pepper to taste, and the bay leaf. Bring to a boil, cover, and simmer 20 minutes.

Strain and reserve the broth. Discard neck and wing tips. Chop the giblets.

Sauté the remaining onion in the butter until tender. Add the rice and cook, stirring, until translucent. Add the reserved broth. Cover and simmer for 20 minutes. Add the giblets and parsley. Bring up to a boil and serve. Serves 4 to 5.

Chicken

CHICKEN DIVAN

4 *spears cooked asparagus or*
  4 stalks cooked broccoli
1 *tablespoon butter or*
  margarine, melted
3 *tablespoons freshly grated*
  Parmesan or Romano
  cheese
⅓ *cup sherry*

4 SLICES LEFTOVER CHICKEN OR
  TURKEY BREAST
2 *egg yolks*
1 *cup medium Sauce*
  Béchamel (page 230)
Salt
Freshly ground white pepper

Preheat oven to 350°.

Arrange the asparagus or broccoli in a shallow baking dish. Sprinkle with the melted butter, 1 tablespoon of the cheese and 2 tablespoons of the sherry. Place the sliced chicken on top and sprinkle with 1 tablespoon of cheese and 2 of the sherry.

Beat the egg yolks, one at a time, into the Sauce Béchamel, beating hard after each addition. Season to taste with salt and pepper. Spoon over the chicken and sprinkle with the remaining cheese and sherry.

Bake for about 12 minutes or until delicately brown. Serves 3, perhaps 4.

CHICKEN PILAF

4 tablespoons (½ stick) butter
  or margarine
1 small yellow onion, peeled
  and minced
¼ cup water
9 to 10 fresh button
  mushrooms (about ¼
  pound)
1 large rib celery (with leaves,
  if any), diced

2½ cups poultry broth
  (page 59)
1 cup long grain rice
Salt
Freshly ground pepper
2 CUPS DICED LEFTOVER
  CHICKEN, OR TURKEY
8 to 10 sprigs parsley, minced

Heat the butter in a heavy skillet or casserole. Add the onion, ¼ cup water, and cook until the onion is soft and the water has boiled away. Add the mushrooms and cook about 3 minutes, stirring occasionally. Stir in the celery and broth. Bring to a boil. Add the rice and salt and pepper to taste. Cover and simmer for 20 minutes or until the rice has absorbed all the liquid. Stir with a fork, then stir in the chicken and parsley. Place on Flame Tamer* to heat thoroughly. Serves about 4.

* See page 61.

CHICKEN SOUFFLÉ

A delicious way to use up bits and pieces of chicken that are
not adequate for anything else.

Butter
½ cup freshly grated
Parmesan cheese (about 2
ounces)
4 whole eggs, separated
2 cups Sauce Velouté
(page 231)*

2 to 3 extra egg whites
Dash cream of tartar
1 to 2 CUPS FINELY DICED
  LEFTOVER CHICKEN MEAT
½ cup heavy cream

Preheat oven to 375°.

Butter a 2-quart soufflé mold and coat with cheese. Dump
any excess back into the measuring cup. Refrigerate.

Add the yolks, one at a time, to the Sauce Velouté, beating
hard after each addition. Take half the sauce (or 1 cup) and
mix with 2 tablespoons of the cheese. Set this aside to use later.
The soufflé can be prepared ahead to this point and set aside,
sealed with plastic wrap.

Beat the egg whites with a dash of salt and cream of tartar
until they hold firm, shiny peaks when the beater is held straight
up. Whip about a third of the whites into the sauce vigorously.
Then mix in the chicken. Pour the mixture over the remaining
whites and fold in very gently with a rubber spatula. Spoon into
the prepared mold, sprinkle with the remaining cheese, place
on a baking sheet and bake for 25 to 30 minutes.

Stir the cream into the remaining cup of Sauce Velouté
and reheat slowly to the boiling point, stirring constantly. Pour
into a warm sauceboat and serve with the soufflé.

---

* Make the Sauce Velouté in these proportions: 6 tablespoons butter or
margarine; 6 tablespoons flour; 2 cups chicken broth; salt, freshly ground
white pepper to taste and freshly grated nutmeg.

OMELET À LA REINE

1 CUP FINELY DICED LEFTOVER
  CHICKEN
2 *tablespoons butter or*
  margarine

1 *omelet (page 150)*
¾ *cup Sauce Suprême*
  (page 232)
Watercress

Heat the chicken in the butter only long enough to heat through. Spread on the cooked omelet just before you fold it. Serve omelet on a warm plate garnished with a ring of hot Sauce Suprême and a bouquet of watercress.

SAUCE ALLA ROMEO FOR SPAGHETTI

2 *tablespoons butter or*
  margarine
2 *tablespoons olive or*
  vegetable oil or half and
  half
1 *medium yellow onion,*
  peeled and chopped fine

½ CUP FINELY CHOPPED
  LEFTOVER CHICKEN
½ *teaspoon dried sage*
½ *teaspoon salt*
½ *cup dry white jug wine*
Grated Parmesan

Heat the butter and oil in a heavy skillet. Add the onion and ½ cup of water and boil until all the water has evaporated and the onion is soft and tender. Add more water if necessary. Stir in the chicken, sage, salt and wine. Bring to a boil. Reduce heat and simmer for 6 to 7 minutes.

Serve hot over freshly cooked spaghetti with grated Parmesan cheese on the side. Serves 4.

CHICKEN, MELON AND
RICE SALAD

¾ CUP CUBED LEFTOVER
   CHICKEN
1 *cup cold boiled rice*
1 *cup cubed melon*
1 *teaspoon chopped chives*

1 *tablespoon butter or*
   margarine
2 *teaspoons curry powder*
1 *cup mayonnaise*

Combine chicken, rice, melon and chives in a bowl. Melt the butter in a small saucepan. When bubbling, stir in the curry powder and simmer for 3 or 4 minutes, stirring constantly. Cool and mix with the mayonnaise.

Pour the mayonnaise over the chicken mixture and mix well. Chill before serving. Serves 3 or 4.

TOMATOES STUFFED WITH
CHICKEN

4 *medium-sized ripe tomatoes*
¼ *pound (6 to 8) fresh button*
   mushrooms, sliced
1 CUP DICED LEFTOVER CHICKEN
Lemon juice
Salt

Freshly ground pepper
¼ *cup mayonnaise*
½ *sweet green pepper, seeds*
   and ribs removed, cut into
   short julienne strips
Lettuce

Prepare tomatoes (see Tomatoes Andalusian, page 183).

To make the stuffing, combine all ingredients except the green pepper and lettuce. Spoon into the tomatoes, slightly mounding the top. Garnish with the julienne of pepper and serve on lettuce. Serves 4.

CHICKEN IN LETTUCE LEAVES
(*In the Chinese Manner*)

3 tablespoons butter or
  margarine
1 yellow onion, peeled and
  minced
½ small green pepper, seeded,
  ribs removed and minced
1½ CUPS FINELY CHOPPED
  LEFTOVER CHICKEN
¾ cup cooked rice
1 teaspoon dried basil
Salt to taste

Several twists of the
  peppermill
Dash Tabasco
¼ cup chicken broth, if
  needed
6 or 8 sprigs parsley, minced
3 or 4 tablespoons toasted
  slivered almonds
1 head crisp, cold iceberg
  lettuce

Melt the butter in a skillet. Add the onion and green pepper and sauté until barely soft. Add the chicken and rice and cook 4 to 5 minutes. Stir in the basil, salt and pepper. Taste. Then add a good splash of Tabasco to give it a hot bite. Stir in the chicken broth, if the mixture seems too dry. Place in a warm bowl garnished with the parsley and almonds; arrange the lettuce leaves in a separate chilled bowl.

Each person serves himself thus: A spoonful or so of the hot chicken is placed on a lettuce leaf, which is then rolled up and eaten out of hand. Serves 4.

CHICKEN LOAF

2 tablespoons butter or
  margarine
5 to 6 button mushrooms,
  sliced
3 tablespoons all-purpose flour
⅔ cup milk
1 cup cooked rice
2 CUPS CHOPPED LEFTOVER
  CHICKEN

Salt
Freshly ground white pepper
1 egg, well beaten
1 cup medium Sauce Velouté
  (page 231)
Paprika
Chopped pimiento

Preheat oven to 350°.

Melt the butter in a saucepan. Add the mushrooms and sauté for 3 to 4 minutes. Lift from the pan with a slotted spoon to paper towels. Stir in the flour until smooth. Cook, stirring, until the mixture froths. Add the milk and beat until the sauce bubbles and thickens. Stir in the rice and chicken. Season well with salt and pepper. Stir in the beaten egg.

Pack into a 5- or 6-cup loaf pan and bake for 35 minutes or until firm and nicely browned.

While the loaf cooks make the Sauce Velouté. Season with paprika and add a couple of tablespoons of chopped pimiento to the sauce before serving.

Once the loaf has cooked allow to stand for about 5 minutes, then turn out on a serving platter. Serve with the Sauce Velouté spooned over the slices. Serves about 6.

CHICKEN, POTATO AND
GREEN BEAN SALAD

This is a good summer salad because you can take the beans, fresh basil, tomatoes and lettuce—maybe even potatoes—straight from your garden.

1½ cups diced cooked
   potatoes
1½ CUPS DICED LEFTOVER
   CHICKEN
1½ cups finely cut cooked
   green beans or cooked peas
3 tablespoons capers, well
   drained

2 tablespoons chopped fresh
   basil
Sauce Vinaigrette (page 229)
Anchovy paste to taste*
4 tomatoes, quartered
Lettuce

Combine all the ingredients except tomatoes and lettuce. Toss
well with the Sauce Vinaigrette. Arrange on lettuce leaves in a
salad bowl and garnish with the tomatoes. Serves 4 to 6.

COLD CUCUMBER SOUP
WITH CHICKEN

1 cucumber, seeded and diced
½ cup sweet cider
½ cup sour cream
½ cup heavy cream
1 CUP DICED LEFTOVER CHICKEN

Salt
Freshly ground white pepper
2 sprigs fresh dill, chopped
   fine
Chopped chives

Purée the cucumber with the cider in an electric food processor
or blender. Mix with the two creams and chicken. Add salt and
pepper to taste. Stir in the dill. Chill.

Serve in chilled soup cups, garnished with chives. Serves
about 4.

* With a wire whip beat anchovy paste to taste into the Sauce Vinaigrette
until smooth.

CHICKEN FRITTERS GRAND'MÈRE

1 cup all-purpose flour
1½ teaspoons salt
¼ teaspoon paprika
Good pinch ground marjoram
2 whole eggs, separated
⅓ cup milk

2 tablespoons dry sherry
1 CUP CHOPPED LEFTOVER
  CHICKEN
1 cup cooked peas
Fat for deep-fat frying
Watercress

Sift together the flour, salt, paprika and marjoram. Beat the egg yolks until thick and creamy, then beat in the milk and wine. Stir into the flour mixture until smooth. Next stir in the chicken and peas.

Beat the egg whites until they hold firm, shiny peaks when the beater is held straight up. Fold gently into the chicken mixture with a rubber spatula.

Heat the fat to 350° to 375° on a candy thermometer. Drop the batter by tablespoons into the hot fat (don't crowd the pan) and fry until lightly browned on all sides. Drain on paper toweling.

Serve on a heated platter lined with a folded linen napkin, and garnish with watercress. Makes a lot (about 20) but you can eat a lot.

CHICKEN CROQUETTES

1½ CUPS MINCED LEFTOVER
  CHICKEN
1 rib celery, minced
¾ cup, approximately, hot
  medium Sauce Velouté
  (page 231)

Fine dry bread crumbs
Vegetable shortening
Sauce Poulette (page 232)

Mix the chicken and celery together thoroughly. Then mix in enough Sauce Velouté to bind the ingredients well. Cool the mixture, then shape into tubes no larger than 1 inch by 1 inch by 2½ inches. Roll in bread crumbs until coated all over. Dry on racks for 15 to 20 minutes.

To fry, heat the shortening in a deep-fat fryer or deep heavy pot until it reaches 375° on a candy thermometer. Fry the croquettes, a few at a time, until golden. Drain on paper towels. Makes about 8 to 10 croquettes. Keep warm in a low oven. Serve with Sauce Poulette.

Turkey

INSTANT TURKEY TONNATO

The number of people you can serve with this recipe will depend on how much turkey you have left over.

2 cups mayonnaise
Lemon juice
Onion juice
1 7-ounce can white tuna
    meat, packed in oil

Anchovy paste
THIN SLICES OF LEFTOVER
    TURKEY
Garnish:
    Cherry tomatoes,
    Black olives

Season the mayonnaise with lemon and onion juice to taste. Drain the tuna, then flake the meat. Add to the mayonnaise with a squeeze of anchovy paste. Cover with plastic wrap and refrigerate for several hours to mellow the flavors.

To serve, arrange thin slices of turkey breast on a platter

and mask with the tuna sauce. Garnish with cherry tomatoes and black olives. Serve with cold parsleyed rice.

TURKEY AMANDINE

2 tablespoons butter or
  margarine
1 tablespoon vegetable or
  peanut oil
½ pound (10 or so) medium
  mushrooms, sliced
2 tablespoons all-purpose
  flour

2 cups poultry broth (page 59)
Salt
Freshly ground pepper
3 CUPS CUBED LEFTOVER
  TURKEY
½ cup toasted slivered
  almonds

Melt the butter and oil in a heavy 1½ quart casserole. Add the mushrooms and cook over moderate heat for 5 minutes. Sprinkle the flour over the mushrooms and cook, stirring constantly, until you have a thick paste, about 3 minutes. Add the broth, stirring constantly. Season to taste with salt and pepper. Bring to a boil, reduce heat and simmer for 10 minutes. Stir in the turkey and almonds. Bring up to a boil again. If sauce seems a bit thick add a few drops more of broth.

Serve on hot parsleyed rice to 4.

TURKEY SWEET POTATO PIE

To quote James A. Beard, from whom I swiped this recipe, it's a "post-holiday wonder." It really is.

Butter or margarine
3 CUPS DICED LEFTOVER TURKEY
3 CUPS LEFTOVER TURKEY
  STUFFING, WELL CRUMBLED
2 eggs
1 cup milk

Salt
Freshly ground pepper
4 tablespoons butter, softened
2 cups cooked mashed sweet
  potatoes
Freshly grated nutmeg

Preheat oven to 375°.

Butter a generous casserole thoroughly and add the well-mixed turkey and stuffing. Beat the eggs and milk together. Season with salt and pepper. Pour over the turkey mixture.

Beat 3 tablespoons of the butter into the mashed sweet potatoes along with salt, pepper and nutmeg to taste. Spread over the turkey and dot with additional butter.

Bake for 35 to 45 minutes. Serve to 6.

TURKEY MORNAY

4 tablespoons butter or
margarine
8 to 10 fresh button
mushrooms, chopped
2½ CUPS DICED LEFTOVER
TURKEY

2½ cups Sauce Mornay (page
231), heated
Salt
Freshly ground pepper
Buttered bread crumbs
Grated cheese (Parmesan,
Swiss or Cheddar)

Butter a 4- to 5-cup casserole well. Set aside.

Melt the remaining butter in a heavy skillet. Add the mushrooms and sauté until lightly browned. Combine the mushrooms, turkey and hot Sauce Mornay. Season to taste with salt and pepper. Pour into the prepared casserole, sprinkle with bread crumbs and cheese.

Slide under the broiler just long enough to brown delicately and melt the cheese. Should serve 4.

TURKEY TETRAZZINI

3 tablespoons butter or
   margarine
1 cup heavy cream
3 slices onion
3 sprigs parsley
1 small bay leaf
1 whole clove
3 tablespoons all-purpose flour
Salt
Freshly ground white pepper

Freshly grated nutmeg
1 CUP DICED LEFTOVER TURKEY
   OR CHICKEN
½ cup chopped, cooked
   spaghetti
½ cup sliced, cooked
   mushrooms
⅓ cup bread crumbs
⅓ cup grated Parmesan
   cheese (about 1 ounce)

Preheat oven to 375°.

Butter a 1½-quart casserole well and set aside.

Combine the cream, onion, parsley, bay leaf and clove in a heavy saucepan and bring to a boil. Strain and discard the vegetables and seasonings. Melt 2 tablespoons of the butter in a heavy skillet. Stir in the flour until smooth. Cook, stirring until the mixture froths, about 3 minutes. Add the strained cream mixture, beating hard with a whip. Bring to a boil, whipping constantly. Season to taste with salt, freshly ground white pepper and nutmeg. Stir in the turkey, spaghetti and mushrooms. Mix well. Pour into the buttered casserole.

Melt the remaining butter and mix with the bread crumbs and cheese. Sprinkle over the mixture in the casserole. Bake until crumbs are golden. Serve at once, bubbling hot.

SCALLOPED TURKEY

3 tablespoons butter or
  margarine
1 12-ounce box of noodles,
  cooked and drained
1 CUP LEFTOVER TURKEY
  STUFFING
2 CUPS DICED LEFTOVER TURKEY
½ pound button mushrooms
  (about 20), sliced

1 small yellow onion, peeled
  and minced
8 to 10 sprigs parsley, minced
8 hard-cooked eggs, peeled
  and sliced
2 cups turkey gravy or Sauce
  Béchamel (page 230)*
Buttered bread crumbs

Preheat oven to 350°.

Butter a deep 2½-quart baking dish and arrange half the cooked noodles on the bottom. Scatter the dressing and turkey over the noodles.

Heat the butter in a heavy skillet. Sauté the mushrooms and the onion, stirring occasionally. Add to the casserole with the parsley and the sliced eggs. Pour the turkey gravy or Sauce Béchamel over and top with the remaining noodles. Dot with butter and sprinkle with the buttered bread crumbs.

Cover and bake for 25 to 30 minutes. Remove the cover and continue baking 10 minutes longer.

Serve with a green salad and a bottle of dry red jug wine.

* Make the Sauce Béchamel in these proportions: 2 tablespoons butter or margarine; 2 tablespoons flour; 2 cups milk; salt, freshly ground white pepper and nutmeg to taste.

Duck

Roast Duck

There is so little meat on most ducks (one 5-pound duck yields
about ¾ to 1 pound of meat) that you are not likely to have
any leftovers, but if you have frozen some livers you can prepare
a nice appetizer and the carcass will, of course, make Duck Soup.

DUCK LIVERS WITH GRAPES

A charming and delicious hors d'oeuvre for two.

2 to 3 LEFTOVER DUCK LIVERS,
   THAWED
Salt
Freshly ground pepper
½ cup dry white wine
2 tablespoons tomato paste
¼ cup water
1 teaspoon meat glaze
Seedless grapes

Preheat oven to 300°.

Cut any fat off the livers. Sprinkle with salt and pepper.
Place in a covered baking dish and bake for 20 minutes. Add the
wine, tomato paste mixed with the water, and the meat glaze.
Heat.

Garnish the dish with grapes and serve to 2.

DUCK SOUP

ROAST DUCK CARCASS*
1 yellow onion, peeled and
    chopped
2 ribs celery, chopped
1 leek, well washed and
    chopped (optional)
2 whole cloves
2 bay leaves

1 cup dry red jug wine
6 cups cold water
1 chicken bouillon cube
1 tablespoon salt
Freshly ground pepper
1/2 cup heavy cream, heated
2 egg yolks

Chop up the carcass and place in a large heavy soup kettle with
all ingredients except the bouillon cube, salt and pepper, cream
and egg yolks. Bring to a boil slowly, reduce heat, cover and
simmer for about 2 hours. Strain the soup and taste for seasoning. You may find it needs salt, freshly ground pepper and the
bouillon cube.

Just before serving, bring the soup up to a boil. Beat the
hot cream and egg yolks together with a whip. Add to the hot
broth, whipping briskly. Serves 6, maybe 8.

CASSOULET

Sturdy French peasant fare, the cassoulet can be made from the
leftovers of a goose or duck. This recipe is an informal version
of the classic dish. Although it sounds complicated, most of
the steps can be done days ahead, even at different times. You
can put it all together and cook it the day you serve it.

* If there was any gravy, dressing or giblets left over from the original
meal, by all means add them to the soup pot.

2 pounds (2 16-ounce
  packages) white pea or
  navy beans
1 tablespoon salt
1 large onion, peeled and
  stuck with 2 whole cloves
1 carrot, peeled and quartered
2 ripe tomatoes, peeled,
  seeded and chopped, or 1
  can (14-ounce size) Italian
  plum tomatoes
3 cloves garlic, crushed and
  peeled
1 bouquet garni tied in a
  cheesecloth bag:
  1 bay leaf, 1 teaspoon dried
  thyme, 4 to 5 sprigs parsley

1 pound lean, cured bacon,
  all in one piece
4 cups poultry broth (page 59)
4 cups cold water
Goose or duck carcass
1 1-pound garlic sausage, such
  as Polish Kielbasa or Genoa
  salami
Freshly ground pepper
1 pound pork shoulder, boned,
  rolled and tied
5 slices bread made into fine
  fresh bread crumbs
½ cup butter or fat, melted

Cover the beans with cold water and allow to soak for 2 to 3 hours. Lift from the water to an 8- to 10-quart heavy enameled casserole with a cover. Add the salt, onion, carrot, tomatoes (if canned, both tomatoes and juice), garlic, the bouquet garni, the bacon, broth and cold water.

If the legs of the duck or goose were not served, cut them off the body and set aside. Using a sharp cleaver, cut up the carcass, leaving any meat that clings to it. Arrange the pieces on top of the beans. Bring up to a boil slowly, reduce heat, cover, and simmer for about 1¼ hours. At this point, pierce the sausage with a fork and add to the casserole. Cook another ½ hour.

Meanwhile, salt and pepper the pork and roast in a preheated 375° oven for 1 hour or until a meat thermometer registers 165° to 170°. Place the legs, if any, in the hot oven just long enough to heat through.

When the beans are cooked (they should be tender but not mushy), take off the heat. Discard the bones, salvaging any meat that still clings to them. Lift out the sausage and bacon from the casserole to a pan and cool slightly. Discard the bouquet garni. Should you find after removing the bones and meats that there is too much liquid, place the casserole over a good heat, bring to a boil, and reduce the liquid somewhat. The beans should not be dry. Combine whatever fat has accumulated from the pork pan with the butter or fat. Set aside.

Prepare the meats to combine with the beans: Slice the meat off the bird's legs; slice the sausage about ¾ inch thick; the bacon in strips about 1½ inches long by 3 inches wide. Slice the pork in half lengthwise, then into 1-inch slices. Add to the casserole and stir well.

Spread the bread crumbs over the entire surface. Spoon the melted fat over them. Place in a preheated 350° oven for about 30 minutes or until a crust has formed on top. Break the crust into the beans with a large spoon and allow it to brown again for another 30 minutes.

The cassoulet can rest, out of the oven, for 20 to 30 minutes before serving. Serve straight from the casserole, accompanied by prepared mustard and lots of dry red jug wine. Serves 8 to 10 generously.

GAME

GAME SOUP WITH LENTILS

1 cup dry lentils
2 whole cloves garlic, crushed
    and peeled
2 bay leaves
7 cups meat (page 10) or
    poultry (page 59) broth
Salt
Freshly ground pepper
QUAIL, VENISON, DUCK, GOOSE
    AND/OR PHEASANT BONES
    AND ANY MEAT CLINGING TO
    THEM
LEFTOVER GRAVY, IF ANY
LEFTOVER DRESSING, IF ANY

1 large onion, peeled and
    sliced
1 large onion, peeled and
    stuck with 3 cloves
1 carrot, washed and sliced
1 cup dry red jug wine
6 juniper berries, crushed
1 teaspoon thyme
1 teaspoon sage
2 tablespoons butter or
    margarine
4 to 5 leftover chicken livers,
    thawed
½ cup Madeira

Wash and pick over the lentils, discarding odds and ends such as seeds, soil or even tiny stones. Drain and add the garlic, bay leaves and 3 cups of broth. Simmer until the lentils are tender to the bite. About an hour. Season with salt and pepper and set aside.

Place whatever carcasses and bones you have in a large soup kettle along with gravy and dressing. Add all the remaining ingredients except the butter, chicken livers and Madeira. Add enough water to just cover. Simmer very gently, covered, for 1½ to 2 hours. Strain. Pick off any meat clinging to the bones and add to the broth. Discard bones and vegetables. Rinse out the kettle, return the broth and add the lentils with their broth.

Heat the butter and brown the livers. Purée with the butter and Madeira in the electric blender. Stir into the soup. Bring the soup to a boil. Serves about 8.

FISH

Storing Fish*

Commercially Frozen "Swimming" Fish

Commercially frozen "swimming" fish (as Jacques Pépin calls them) should be placed in a freezer (which should maintain *zero* temperature or below) in its *unopened* package immediately after you get it home—unless, of course, it is going to be thawed for cooking. Fish stored at temperatures above zero lose color, flavor, texture and nutritional value.

Fat fish (Lake trout, mackerel, mullet, salmon, sea herring, shad, tuna and whitefish) will keep three months; *lean fish* (catfish, cod, croaker, flounder, grouper, haddock, hake, halibut, lake perch, ocean perch, pollack, rainbow trout, red snapper, sea bass, striped bass, sea trout, sole, swordfish and whiting) will keep six months.

Commercially Frozen Shellfish

Commercially frozen shellfish should be handled exactly the way you do "swimming" fish. That is, placed in the freezer, at *zero* (or below) temperature, in its unopened package immediately you get the shellfish home. Lobster and crabmeat will keep two months; shrimp, six months; oysters, scallops and shucked clams, three to four months.

* Information from the National Fisheries Institute.

Storing Home-frozen Fish

Freezing *store-bought* fresh fish is not recommended. However, freshly caught fish (and note the words "freshly caught") can be frozen and stored in the home freezer. Fish should be eviscerated and washed soon after being caught Then it should be wrapped in moisture-vapor-proof material and packed tightly to exclude air. Heavy aluminum, vapor-proof cellophane, pliofilm, polyethylene or laminated freezer paper are satisfactory packaging materials. The fish should be frozen quickly at minus 10 degrees Fahrenheit, but once frozen, can be stored at *zero* temperature or below. Fat fish (see above) will keep safely for three months; lean (see above) for six months.

Storing Home-frozen Fresh Shellfish

Freezing store-bought shellfish is not recommended, and on the whole, it is not practical to freeze shellfish you've caught yourself.

Freezing and Storing Cooked Shellfish

When you've cooked more shellfish than you can eat, shuck (if necessary), clean and chill. Place in a pint container and cover with chilled fish broth (see page 99), or poultry broth (page 59). Cover tightly to seal out air and seal in moisture. Label. Freeze solid at minus 10 degrees Fahrenheit. Store at *zero* temperature. Use within 10 days.

Thawing Frozen Fish and Shellfish

Any kind of frozen fish or shellfish should be thawed in the refrigerator. (Allow 24 hours for a 1-pound package). However, thawing can be speeded up by placing the package, intact, under cold running water for 1 to 2 hours. Once thawed, the fish should be used within 24 hours.

Smoked Fish

Smoked fish will keep refrigerated up to one week. The smoking process only enhances the flavor, it is not sufficient to preserve the fish.

Fish Bones

FISH BROTH

Whenever you buy a piece of fish, ask the fish man to give you all the bones, and if possible the head. If he's a generous soul he'll throw in some extra bones. (However, things being what they are, he may charge you. Whatever, get the bones.) Remember Sauce Velouté (page 231) is made with fish broth to serve with fish dishes. It is also used to make fish soufflés.

2 POUNDS FISH BONES AND
   TRIMMINGS
Cold water to cover
1 large yellow onion, unpeeled,
   quartered
1 or 2 ribs celery, chopped
1 large carrot, washed and
   chopped

1 cup dry white jug wine
4 cups cold water
2 or 3 sprigs parsley
1 bay leaf
½ teaspoon dried thyme
Salt to taste

Place the fish bones and trimmings in a generous kettle. Cover with cold water. Bring to a boil. Strain and discard the water. Rinse out the kettle and rinse the bones in cold water. This gets rid of the scum.

Return the bones to the kettle with all remaining ingredients. Bring to a boil, reduce heat, and simmer for about 30 minutes. Strain through a large sieve lined with several layers of dampened cheesecloth. Makes about 1½ quarts. Freeze in 1-pint jars.

JACQUES PÉPIN'S
SOUPE DE POISSON

(*Fish Soup*)

One of those wonderful hearty soups everybody loves that are
so delicious on a cold night. It couldn't be less expensive, but
what gives this soup its marvelous flavor is the combination of
the fish broth with the vegetables and the aromatic herbs all
cooked together. It's made in three steps.

Step One

1 *big yellow onion, peeled
and diced fine*
1 *leek, thoroughly washed,
with about 2 inches of the
green part, diced fine
(optional)*

1 *rib celery, diced fine*
½ *cup parsley sprigs, minced*
½ *cup fennel, diced, or 1
teaspoon fennel seeds,
crushed*
2 *carrots, scrubbed and diced*
4 *tablespoons olive oil*

Heat the oil in a heavy 8- to 10-quart kettle. When hot, add the
vegetables and herbs. Cook together for about 5 minutes, giving
the mixture an occasional stir.

Step Two. Add:

6 *cloves garlic, crushed and
peeled*
2 *or 3 very ripe tomatoes, cut
in chunks, or 1 can (14½-
ounce size) whole peeled
tomatoes, with the juices*
3 *bay leaves*

Big pinch saffron
1½ *tablespoons salt*
Freshly ground black pepper
3 to 4 POUNDS FISH HEADS
(GILLS REMOVED) AND
BONES, WASHED
THOROUGHLY

Mix together and cook 3 minutes longer

Step Three

½ *cup tomato purée*   *4 cups cold water*
2 *cups dry white jug wine*

Bring up to a boil, cover and cook over high heat for 25 minutes. Discard all the bones. Then push the mixture through a food mill. Makes about 2 quarts of soup, which, with the garnish, will serve 8 to 10.

Garnish: Cook 4 Idaho potatoes in boiling salted water until tender when pierced with a sharp paring knife. Drain. When cool enough to handle, peel and slice fairly thick. Set aside. Keep warm in a little of the hot broth.

Take about 8 to 10 slices firm white bread. Cut into squares and brush both sides with olive oil (takes about 1 cup). Place on a baking sheet in a preheated 375° oven until brown—20 to 25 minutes. When cold, rub each crouton with the split side of a garlic clove.

To serve: Place slices of the baked potato and the croutons in large soup plates. Fill the plates with the boiling soup. Serve at once.

SAUCE BERCY

2 CUPS FISH BROTH (PAGE 99)   *Freshly ground white pepper*
5 *or 6 green onion bulbs,*   ½ *cup dry white jug wine*
  chopped fine   6 *tablespoons (¾ stick) butter*
5 *or 6 sprigs parsley, chopped*   *or margarine*
  fine   3 *tablespoons all-purpose flour*
Salt

Combine the fish broth, onions, half the parsley, salt, pepper and wine in a saucepan. Place over a high heat and bring to a boil. Reduce (that is, boil down) the sauce until you have about two-thirds left.

Melt 4 tablespoons of the butter, stir in the flour and cook over medium heat, stirring constantly for 3 minutes or so. Do not allow it to brown. Add the broth and cook, whipping occasionally, for 10 to 15 minutes. Stir in the remaining butter and parsley. Makes about 3 cups. Pour into a heated sauceboat. Serve with fish.

Fish Recipes

FISH CROQUETTES

1½ CUPS FLAKED LEFTOVER
  FISH
1 rib celery, minced
¾ cup hot medium Sauce
  Velouté (page 233)

Fine dry bread crumbs
Vegetable shortening
Sauce Tartare (page 231) or
  Tomato Sauce (page 235)

Mix the fish and celery together thoroughly. Then mix in enough Sauce Velouté to bind the ingredients well. Cool the mixture, then shape into tubes no larger than 1 inch by 1 inch by 2½ inches. Roll in bread crumbs until coated all over. Dry on racks for 15 to 20 minutes.

To fry, heat the shortening in a deep-fat fryer or deep heavy pot until it reaches 400° on a candy thermometer. Fry the croquettes, a few at a time, until golden. Drain on paper towels. Makes about 8 to 10 croquettes. Keep warm in a low oven. Serve with Tartare Sauce, Tomato Sauce or lemon quarters.

FISH PUDDING

4 tablespoons (½ stick) butter
  or margarine, melted
4 CUPS FLAKED LEFTOVER FISH
2 cups plain mashed potatoes
1 teaspoon salt

Freshly ground white pepper
5 or 6 sprigs parsley, minced
1 egg
½ cup light cream
Sauce Bercy (page 101)

Preheat oven to 350°.

Butter a 1½-quart baking dish or casserole. Set aside.

Mix the fish and potatoes together. Stir in the remaining melted butter, salt, pepper to taste and parsley. Mix well.

Beat the egg and cream together and stir into the mixture. Spoon into the prepared casserole and bake for 30 minutes.

Serve to 4, with Sauce Bercy.

FISH BALLS

2 CUPS FLAKED LEFTOVER FISH
2 cups mashed potatoes
1 teaspoon grated onion
1 teaspoon dried thyme
8 to 10 sprigs parsley, minced
3 eggs
Salt

Freshly ground pepper
Juice of ½ lemon
Fine dry bread crumbs
  page (197)
Fat for deep frying
Lemon wedges
Tomato Sauce (page 233)

Combine fish, potatoes, onion, thyme, parsley, 2 of the eggs, lightly beaten, salt and pepper to taste and lemon juice. Mix well (best done with your hands). Shape into 2-inch balls. Beat the remaining egg with 1 tablespoon of water. Dip the balls into the egg mixture, then roll in the bread crumbs. Place on racks to dry for 15 to 20 minutes.

Fry in deep fat, heated to 375° on a candy thermometer, until golden. Drain on paper towels. Makes about 3 dozen.

Arrange on a heated serving dish and garnish with lemon wedges. Serve with Tomato Sauce.

FISH SOUFFLÉ

3 tablespoons butter or
  margarine
2 yellow onions, peeled and
  minced
1 cup cold water
1 clove garlic, crushed, peeled
  and minced

2 cups mashed potatoes
1½ CUPS FLAKED LEFTOVER FISH
Salt
Freshly ground pepper
4 eggs, separated
2 extra egg whites
Mustard Sauce (page 231)

Preheat oven to 375°.

Butter a 1½-quart soufflé dish well, including the curve at the bottom. Refrigerate.

Melt the remaining butter in a skillet, add the onions and water. Bring to a boil and continue to boil until all the water has evaporated and the onions are cooked and soft. Add the garlic and mix thoroughly with the potatoes and fish. Season well with salt and pepper. Beat the egg yolks lightly, then stir into the fish mixture.

Beat the whites until they hold firm, shiny peaks when the beater is held straight up. With a wire whip, beat about a third into the fish mixture. Pour over the remaining whites and fold in gently with a rubber spatula. Pour into the prepared mold.

Place on a baking sheet in oven and bake for 30 minutes. Serve at once with Mustard Sauce.

SALMON SOUFFLÉ

4 tablespoons butter

3 tablespoons all-purpose flour

¾ cup milk

Salt

4 whole eggs, separated

1 CUP FLAKED LEFTOVER
  SALMON

Juice of ½ lemon, strained

½ teaspoon dried tarragon

2 extra egg whites

Hollandaise Sauce (page 146)

Preheat oven to 375°.

Butter a 1½-quart soufflé mold, including the curve at the bottom. Refrigerate.

Melt the remaining butter in a heavy saucepan. Stir in the flour until smooth. Cook, over moderate heat, stirring constantly until the mixture froths, about 3 minutes. Add the milk and beat with a wire whip until the sauce thickens. Season to taste with salt.

Add the egg yolks, one at a time, beating hard after each addition. Stir in the salmon, lemon juice and tarragon.

Beat the egg whites until they hold firm, shiny peaks when the beater is held straight up. Beat about a third into the salmon mixture. Pour over the remaining whites and fold in gently with a rubber spatula.

Pour into the prepared mold and place on a baking sheet. Bake for 35 to 40 minutes or until lightly browned. Serve with Hollandaise Sauce.

FISH HASH

2 tablespoons bacon fat

1 small yellow onion, peeled
  and minced

2 CUPS FLAKED LEFTOVER FISH

2 cups diced cooked potatoes

2 hard-cooked eggs, peeled
  and diced

⅔ cup milk

Salt

Freshly ground white pepper

Worcestershire sauce

Melt the fat in a heavy skillet. Add the onion and cook over moderate heat until golden.

Combine the fish, potatoes and eggs in a generous bowl. In a measuring cup, mix milk with salt, pepper and Worcestershire to taste. Pour over the fish mixture and mix lightly.

Turn into the skillet and smooth with a spatula. Cover and cook over moderate heat until crusty and brown on the bottom. Using a pancake turner, turn half the hash over the other half. Serve at once to about 5.

FISH SOUP

2 tablespoons butter or
  margarine
½ yellow onion, peeled and
  minced
1 cup milk
1 CUP FLAKED LEFTOVER FISH

2 cups Sauce Velouté (page
  231)*
Salt
Freshly ground white pepper
Freshly grated nutmeg
Minced parsley

Place butter in a heavy saucepan, add onion and milk. Bring to a boil and simmer for 10 to 15 minutes, or until onion is soft.

Purée the fish, about half at a time, in the container of an electric blender with part of the milk and onion mixture. Combine in a saucepan with remaining milk and the Sauce Velouté. Bring to a boil. Season to taste with salt, pepper and nutmeg. Garnish with parsley, and serve to 4 or 5.

* Make the Sauce Velouté in these proportions: 3 tablespoons butter or margarine; 3 tablespoons flour; 2 cups fish broth; salt and pepper to taste.

FISH DUMPLINGS

Fish dumplings make an attractive garnish for a fish platter or fish soup. But they can also be served as a main course with a sauce.

1 tablespoon butter or
    margarine
2 tablespoons all-purpose
    flour
⅓ cup hot milk
Salt
Freshly ground pepper
Freshly ground nutmeg
Dash ground cloves

Good pinch thyme
2 egg yolks
1½ tablespoons dry sherry
1½ CUPS FLAKED LEFTOVER FISH
4 tablespoons fine dry
    cracker crumbs
Fish broth (page 99)
Sauce Velouté (page 231) or
    Hollandaise (page 146)

Melt the butter in a heavy saucepan over low heat. Stir in the flour until smooth. Cook until the mixture froths, 2 to 3 minutes. Add the milk and cook, beating constantly with a wire whip, until the mixture comes to a boil and thickens. Reduce heat, place on a Flame Tamer (page 61) or asbestos pad and simmer for 5 minutes, stirring occasionally. Season to taste with salt, pepper, nutmeg, cloves and thyme. Cool slightly. Then beat in the egg yolks, one at a time, beating hard after each addition. Beat in the sherry. Then add the fish alternately with the cracker crumbs.

Shape into about 8 dumplings. Drop into boiling salted fish broth a few at a time. Cook until the dumplings rise to the surface. Drain on paper towels and serve at once with Sauce Velouté, or Hollandaise.

FISH SALAD

Flaked leftover sole or
   halibut
Cherry tomatoes, stemmed
Sliced white onions

Black olives
Sauce Vinaigrette (page 229)
Lettuce leaves

Combine all ingredients except the last two. Mix with Sauce
Vinaigrette. Serve chilled on a bed of lettuce.

WHITE FISH WITH CHEESE SAUCE

3 tablespoons butter or
   margarine (approximately)
2 tablespoons all-purpose flour
1 cup fish broth (page 99)
1 cup half and half
Salt
Freshly ground white pepper
Freshly ground nutmeg

4 tablespoons grated Parmesan
   or Gruyère cheese
2 CUPS FLAKED, LEFTOVER FISH
About 2 small cooked
   potatoes, peeled and sliced
   thin
Fine dry bread crumbs

Preheat oven to 400°.

Melt 2 tablespoons of the butter in a heavy saucepan. Stir
in the flour and cook, stirring constantly, until it froths, about
3 minutes. Do not brown. Add the broth and half and half,
beating constantly with a whip. Cook, whipping, over moderate
heat until the sauce thickens lightly. Season to taste with salt,
pepper and nutmeg. Place a Flame Tamer (page 61) or asbestos
mat under the skillet and simmer for 15 minutes, stirring occasionally. Finally, stir in the cheese.

Coat the bottom of a flat 6-inch by 10-inch baking dish that
can go to the table with some of the cheese sauce. Place the fish,
crumbled, on top and arrange a ring of potatoes around the
edge. Pour the remaining sauce over all the fish and potatoes.

Sprinkle with bread crumbs and dot with little nuts of the remaining butter. Bake about 10 minutes. Then slide under the broiler for a few seconds. Will probably serve 4 or 5.

COD LOAF

Butter or margarine
1 CUP FLAKED LEFTOVER FRESH
   COD
*½ small yellow onion, peeled
   and chopped fine*
½ rib celery, minced
*½ green pepper, seeded, ribs
   removed, chopped fine*
6 to 8 sprigs parsley, minced

*½ cup fine toasted bread
   crumbs*
Salt
Freshly ground white pepper
½ teaspoon dried tarragon
1 egg, separated
¼ cup milk
2 tablespoons butter, melted
Egg Sauce (page 232)

Preheat oven to 375°.

Butter a 3-cup mold or loaf pan. Set aside.

Mix together all ingredients except the egg, milk and melted butter.

Beat the egg yolk. Then stir into the fish mixture with the milk and melted butter. Beat the egg white until it holds firm, shiny peaks when the beater is held straight up, then fold into the fish mixture. Pour into the prepared mold. Place in a baking pan. Add enough hot water from the tap to reach to two-thirds the depth of the mold.

Bake for about 40 minutes or until set. Turn out on a heated platter and serve with Egg Sauce to 4 or 5.

CODFISH CAKES

In Canada we always served our fish cakes with homemade apple sauce. Good, too.

1 CUP SHREDDED LEFTOVER SALT   *Freshly ground white pepper*
   CODFISH   *Butter, margarine or bacon*
1 *cup mashed potatoes*   *fat*
1 *egg*

Mix the codfish, potatoes, egg and pepper together. Shape into cakes. Sauté in butter in a heavy skillet until golden on both sides. Makes about 6 cakes.

SALT COD IN SCALLOP SHELLS

Here as in other instances, the proportions are up to you. It is not too difficult, really, to prepare a dish without precise measurements.

Medium Sauce Béchamel   *Several mushrooms, minced*
   (page 230)   *Butter*
Grated cheese   *Bread crumbs*
FLAKED LEFTOVER SALT COD

Preheat oven to 375°.

   To Sauce Béchamel add some grated cheese, the cod and the mushrooms. Butter scallop shells, fill with the mixture and smooth the surface. Sprinkle with grated cheese and bread crumbs. Bake until bubbling and golden.

FINNAN HADDIE CASSEROLE

1½ cups hot Sauce Béchamel   6 stuffed olives, chopped
    (page 230)*   3 hard-cooked eggs, sliced
2 CUPS FLAKED LEFTOVER   2 teaspoons onion juice
    FINNAN HADDIE   Grated cheese
1 pimiento, chopped

Butter a 4-cup baking dish thoroughly. Set aside.

Make the Sauce Béchamel in the proportions given below, then add all ingredients. Place over moderate heat until the mixture comes to a boil. Pour into the prepared dish and slide under a preheated broiler just long enough to melt the cheese and brown the top a bit. Serves 4 or 5.

* Make the Sauce Béchamel in these proportions: 2 tablespoons butter or margarine; 2 tablespoons flour; 1½ cups milk; salt and freshly ground pepper to taste.

DAIRY
PRODUCTS

Storing Dairy Products

Where and How Long Can You Store Milk and Cream?

The USDA says: Fresh milk, cream and milk products should be refrigerated as soon as possible after purchase. For best flavor, milk and cream should be used within 3 to 5 days; dry *whole* milk within a few weeks; reconstituted dry milk within 3 to 5 days; whipped cream in an aerosol can within a few weeks. Evaporated milk, unopened, can be stored at room temperature and used within 6 months (if opened, use within 3 to 5 days); *nonfat* dry milk can be stored at room temperature, tightly covered, and should be used within a few months.

To Freeze Heavy Cream

If you haven't used up a carton of heavy cream—say, by the end of a week—you can freeze it in its own container. When you are ready to use it, partially thaw, then whip. It cannot be used except for whipping.

Storing Sour Cream, Yoghurt and Cottage Cheese

You can keep opened containers of commercial sour cream, yoghurt and cottage cheese longer if you store the cartons upside down. No air gets in because the weight of the contents against the lid keeps it out.

SPANISH NATA* OR A
HAPPY ACCIDENT

My friend Charlotte Mayerson whipped some heavy cream and for some reason had a surplus. Being a thrifty soul, she added some chocolate syrup to the surplus to give it color and flavor, and placed it—still in the glass mixing bowl—in the freezer.

When it was half frozen, she whipped it once more. The result, she said, and we quote, was "like a very suave ice cream." Successful on this roundelay, she tried substituting strawberry purée and fresh sliced strawberries. Superb! Success having gone to her head, she melted some semisweet chocolate and added it, still hot, to the whipped cream which resulted in an "ice cream" with sweet chocolate chips.

Freeze the cream in a china or glass bowl, not in metal. Let it thaw outside the freezer for 10 or 15 minutes before serving.

SOUR CREAM DRESSING I

1 teaspoon dry mustard   *1 cup mayonnaise*
½ CUP LEFTOVER SOUR CREAM

Mix mustard into sour cream. Stir into mayonnaise. Serve with hard-cooked eggs or cold, cooked vegetables.

SOUR CREAM DRESSING II

Here is another recipe where you can use your own judgment and taste to fill in the quantities.

* *Nata* is the Spanish equivalent of American whipped cream.

Mayonnaise　　　　　　　　　*Dry mustard*
LEFTOVER SOUR CREAM　　　　*Salt*
Lemon juice　　　　　　　　　*Freshly ground white pepper*
Sugar

Combine mayonnaise with sour cream and lemon juice to taste. Then stir in sugar, dry mustard, salt and freshly ground white pepper to taste.

ROQUEFORT BISCUITS

2 cups all-purpose flour　　　　*2 tablespoons cold butter or*
½ teaspoon salt　　　　　　　　　*margarine, cut into pieces*
3 teaspoons baking powder　　*⅔ cup milk*
1½ OUNCES ROQUEFORT CHEESE
　(ABOUT 4 TABLESPOONS),
　CRUMBLED

Preheat oven to 425°.

Mix flour, salt and baking powder together in a generous mixing bowl. Add the cheese and the butter and cut into the flour mixture with a pastry blender or two knives until it has the consistency of corn meal. Gradually add the milk, mixing it in with a fork.

Turn out on a floured pastry cloth or board and knead briefly. Roll out (preferably with a rolling pin encased in a sleeve) about ½ inch thick. Cut with a 1½-inch cookie cutter. Place on a baking sheet.

Bake for 12 to 15 minutes. Makes about 2 dozen biscuits.

Serve heated, if you like, split and buttered, along with a salad or with hot or cold soup. Nice, too, with a cocktail.

THREE SALAD DRESSINGS
WITH LEFTOVER ROQUEFORT

A small amount of a sharp, crumbly cheese that can no longer be served makes a lovely flavoring. You can use blue cheese, Gorgonzola or any pungent and crumbly cheese in these recipes.

Creamy Dressing

2 TABLESPOONS CRUMBLED LEFTOVER SHARP CHEESE
½ cup sour cream
1 teaspoon vinegar
½ teaspoon salt
Few twists of the peppermill
½ teaspoon dried tarragon
3 or 4 sprigs parsley, minced

Place all the ingredients in a bowl and mix well. Makes enough dressing for a salad for about 4.

Sharp Cheese Salad Dressing I

⅔ cup peanut or vegetable oil
¼ cup wine vinegar
1 medium bay leaf, crumbled
3 TABLESPOONS CRUMBLED LEFTOVER SHARP CHEESE
1 tablespoon onion juice

Combine all the ingredients in a jar and shake well. Very good on shellfish or vegetable salads. Makes about 1½ cups.

Sharp Cheese Salad Dressing II

1 teaspoon Dijon mustard
1 teaspoon salt
Several twists of the peppermill
1 tablespoon vinegar or lemon juice
½ cup peanut or vegetable oil
2 TABLESPOONS CRUMBLED LEFTOVER SHARP CHEESE

Place the mustard, salt, pepper and vinegar in the salad bowl. Beat with a whip until well amalgamated and somewhat thickened. Add the oil, beating constantly. Then thoroughly mix in the cheese. Makes about ¾ cup.

CHEESE DIP

LEFTOVER CREAM CHEESE, AT   *Paprika*
   ROOM TEMPERATURE   *Chopped chives*
Milk   *Capers, drained and chopped*
Anchovy paste

Take whatever cream cheese you have and beat into it enough milk to make it of dip consistency. Season with anchovy paste, paprika, chives and capers to taste. Serve with unseasoned crackers.

Cottage Cheese Salad Dressing or Dip

When cottage cheese has been kept too long it tastes somewhat acid. You can turn this to an advantage by whipping it hard, then stirring in minced onions, minced parsley and minced fresh herbs to taste.

How to Use Up Dried-out Cheese

If you have a piece of cheese that has become dried out and hard, grate it or pulverize it in the blender. Add it to scrambled eggs, sprinkle it over vegetables, stir it into a cheese soufflé or scalloped potatoes, sprinkle it on pastry fingers (page 203) before baking, add to the pastry for an apple pie, garnish soups with it or use wherever grated cheese is called for.

Soured Milk or Cream

Don't pour soured milk or cream down the drain. If it is just beginning to turn, you can salvage it with a pinch of baking soda. In which case use it up immediately. But if it's really sour it can be used in the following recipes.

SOUR MILK PANCAKES

1 cup all-purpose flour   1 egg
1 teaspoon sugar   1 CUP SOUR MILK
½ teaspoon salt   2 tablespoons butter or
¾ teaspoon baking powder   margarine, melted
½ teaspoon baking soda

Sift all the dry ingredients together. Beat the egg slightly, then beat in the sour milk. Combine the two mixtures and the butter. Pour into the container of an electric blender and blend at top speed for 1 minute. If you don't want to use the batter at once cover and refrigerate for several hours or even overnight. Makes about 10 4-inch cakes.

To bake the pancakes: If you are using an electric skillet or griddle follow the manufacturer's directions. Otherwise, heat the griddle or frying pan over moderate heat (most modern griddles don't need greasing), and if necessary, grease lightly with fat. To test the griddle for correct heat, let a few drops of cold water fall on the pan. When the water bounces and sputters, the griddle is ready to use. To make pancakes all the same size, use a ¼-cup measure. Cook until bubbles appear on the surface, from 2 to 3 minutes. Before bubbles break, lift with a pancake turner or spatula and brown the other side—about 1 minute. *Note:* the second side never browns evenly.

Pancakes should be served immediately, but they can be kept warm in a 200° oven on a dish towel. Do not stack them unless there is a cloth between each one or they will be flabby.

Serve with lots of melted butter or margarine and warm maple syrup.

SOUR MILK WAFFLES

1½ cups all-purpose flour
3 teaspoons baking powder
2 teaspoons sugar
½ teaspoon salt
¼ teaspoon baking soda

1¼ CUPS SOUR MILK, SOUR
   CREAM OR BUTTERMILK
2 eggs
3 tablespoons melted butter,
   margarine or vegetable oil

Sift the dry ingredients together. Beat the sour milk, eggs and butter with a rotary or electric beater. Add the flour mixture and beat hard. If the batter is thicker than heavy cream add a little more milk to thin it. A thin batter makes tender waffles. Pour into a pitcher.

To cook: Heat the waffle iron but do not grease it. Pour enough batter to cover the grid surface about two-thirds full. Close the lid and wait about 4 minutes. When the waffle is cooked, all steam will have stopped emerging from the crack of the iron. If the top of the iron doesn't come up easily it probably means the waffle is not quite done. Give it another minute or so and try again. Makes 6 to 8.

Serve with melted butter or margarine and warm maple syrup, honey, molasses, apple butter or confectioners' sugar.

CINNAMON HONEY MUFFINS

5 tablespoons butter or
   margarine, melted
1 egg, well beaten
1 CUP SOUR MILK, TEPID
2 cups all-purpose flour
1 teaspoon baking powder

½ teaspoon baking soda
½ teaspoon salt
3 tablespoons sugar
1 heaping tablespoon
   cinnamon
Honey

Preheat oven to 400°.

Brush 15 small muffin cups with melted butter. Place in the oven to warm.

Mix the egg, sour milk and remaining butter together and beat well. Combine all remaining ingredients except the honey in a sifter and sift over the egg and milk mixture. Stir just enough to dampen the flour (overmixing is fatal to muffins).

Fill the hot muffin cups ⅔ full and bake for 25 to 30 minutes or until the muffins are brown, firm and leave the sides of the pans. Take from the oven and arrange on a heated platter. Spoon a tablespoon of honey over each muffin. Serve hot.

DELICIOUS DIP FOR STRAWBERRIES

1 CUP SOURED CREAM
Grated rind of ½ lemon
Juice of ½ lemon

½ cup sifted confectioners' sugar

Combine all the ingredients in a bowl and beat with a rotary or electric beater until light and fluffy. Place in a handsome bowl on a platter and surround with strawberries, caps and stems still intact.

SOURED CREAM GINGERBREAD

If a half cup of heavy cream has gone sour on you here's one delicious solution.

Butter
2 eggs
½ CUP SOURED HEAVY CREAM
½ cup molasses
½ cup brown sugar,* firmly
    packed

1½ cups all-purpose flour
1 teaspoon baking soda
1 teaspoon powdered ginger
¼ teaspoon salt
4 tablespoons (½ stick)
    butter, melted (optional)

* If your sugar has hardened on you, a propensity of brown sugar, break up and pulverize in an electric blender.

Preheat oven to 350°.

Line a 9-inch-square baking pan with kitchen parchment. Set aside.

Beat the eggs in a large bowl until thick and creamy. Then beat in the soured cream, molasses and sugar thoroughly. Sift the flour, soda, ginger and salt together. Sift into the egg mixture and stir well. If you want a somewhat richer cake that keeps moist for days stir in the melted butter.

Pour into the prepared pan and bake for 30 minutes or until a toothpick inserted in the center of the cake comes out dry and the cake shrinks slightly from the sides of the pan. Cool for a few minutes on a cake rack. Then slide a knife around the sides and turn out on the rack to cool thoroughly. Discard paper.

SOURED CREAM ORANGE CAKE

*4 tablespoons (½ stick) butter
  or margarine*
2½ cups all-purpose flour
1 cup raisins
*1 medium navel orange, cut
  up (seeds, if any, removed)*

1 cup sugar
2 eggs
1 CUP SOURED CREAM
1 teaspoon baking soda
Whipped cream

Preheat oven to 350°.

Cover the bottom of a 9-inch-square baking pan with a piece of kitchen parchment, or butter and dust with flour. Set aside.

Put the raisins and orange through a food chopper or grind in an electric food processor. Cream the remaining butter and sugar with an electric beater until thick and creamy. Beat in the eggs. Stir in the soured cream, raisins, orange and any juice. Place the remaining flour in sifter, add baking soda and sift over the mixture. Stir in well.

Pour into the prepared pan and bake for 35 minutes or until

a toothpick plunged in the center comes out clean and the cake begins to pull away from the sides of the pan.

Serve warm or at room temperature with whipped cream.

Melted Ice Cream

This makes a flawless sauce to serve over fresh strawberries, peaches, raspberries, blueberries.

EGGS

Egg Whites

Frozen Egg Whites Are Like Money in the Bank

When you've made something that calls for yolks only, mayonnaise or Hollandaise perhaps, freeze the whites to use later on for meringues, angel cake, soufflés, etc.

One egg white fits neatly into a plastic midget freezer container, or individual ice-cube containers. It is the ideal way to freeze them. This also makes it easy to tell at a glance how many whites you have on hand. Once frozen, take the cubes from the container and place in a freezer bag, tied securely. Thaw and use exactly as you would fresh egg whites.

OLD-FASHIONED WHITE FROSTING

2 cups sugar
1 cup water
2 LEFTOVER EGG WHITES

⅛ teaspoon salt
⅛ teaspoon cream of tartar
1 teaspoon vanilla

Combine the sugar and water in a saucepan. Cover, bring to a boil, and cook for 3 minutes. Uncover and cook until it reaches 238° or 240° on a candy thermometer, or syrup dripped from the tip of a spoon makes fine threads.

Beat the egg whites with salt and cream of tartar until frothy. Gradually add the syrup, beating constantly, until you have a shiny frosting that holds firm peaks. Stir in the vanilla.

Makes enough to frost between layers, sides and tops of two 9-inch cake layers.

BROWN SUGAR FROSTING

2 LEFTOVER EGG WHITES
1½ cups dark brown sugar, firmly packed

⅓ cup water
1 teaspoon vanilla

Mix all ingredients except vanilla in the top of double boiler until smooth. Place over briskly boiling water and beat vigorously for 7 minutes with a rotary beater, or 4 minutes with an electric one. Frosting at this point looks fluffy and holds a soft shape.

Take off the heat and stir in the vanilla. Continue beating until the mixture holds a precise point when you lift up the beater. Spread frosting between layers, around sides and over the top of cake.

Makes enough to frost two 9-inch cake layers.

Sea Foam Frosting
To make this frosting, use only 1 cup dark brown sugar and ½ cup granulated sugar.

NORWEGIAN CHOCOLATE MERINGUES

Neither candy nor cookie, these charming little morsels are delicious with coffee.

2½ cups sifted confectioners' sugar

2 tablespoons cocoa
2 LEFTOVER EGG WHITES

Preheat oven to 375°.

Place all the ingredients in the bowl of an electric mixer and beat at high speed until you have a very stiff dough. Roll out on a pastry cloth dusted with confectioners' sugar (use a sleeve on the rolling pin) about ⅓-inch thick. Use extra sugar if the dough sticks.

Cut into 1-inch rounds and place on a baking sheet lined with kitchen parchment, or greased and floured lightly. Bake 10 minutes or until the meringues have puffed. Makes about 24.

SPINACH SOUFFLÉ

Butter or margarine
4 eggs, separated
Sauce Béchamel (page 230)*

2 LEFTOVER EGG WHITES
1 cup cooked chopped
  spinach, squeezed dry

Preheat oven to 375°.

Butter a 1½-quart soufflé dish, including the curve at the bottom. Refrigerate.

Add the egg yolks, one at a time, to the Sauce Béchamel, beating hard after each addition. Stir in the spinach. The soufflé can be prepared ahead to this point, set aside and sealed with plastic wrap.

Beat the egg whites until they hold firm, shiny peaks when the beater is held straight up. Beat about a third into the spinach mixture. Add to the remaining whites and fold in gently with a rubber spatula. Pour into the soufflé dish.

Place on a baking sheet and bake for 35 to 40 minutes. Serve immediately.

* Make the Sauce Béchamel in these proportions: 3 tablespoons butter or margarine; 3 tablespoons flour; 1 cup milk; salt and freshly ground pepper to taste; a pinch each of cayenne and freshly grated nutmeg.

MERINGUES

3 LEFTOVER EGG WHITES   *Big pinch cream of tartar*
Big pinch salt   *¾ cup sugar*

Preheat oven to 275°.

Cover a baking sheet with kitchen parchment or grease, and coat with flour.

Beat the egg whites with the salt and cream of tartar with an electric beater or in the mixer until they begin to hold a shape. Gradually add the sugar in a thin, steady stream, beating hard and constantly until the meringue is stiff and holds shiny peaks when the beater is held straight up. Spoon onto the prepared baking sheet with a tablespoon, leaving space for spreading. Bake for 35 to 40 minutes or until firm to the touch.

Once cooked, lift immediately to a wire rack to cool. Makes 10 to 12 meringues, which keep well if stored in an airtight container.

To serve, place a big dollop of ice cream or sweetened whipped cream between two meringues.

MACAROONS

Almond

¾ cup whole almonds or   3 LEFTOVER EGG WHITES
   1¼ cups grated or ground *1 tablespoon almond extract*
¾ cup sugar

Preheat oven to 300°.

---

* Filberts or Brazil nuts may be used instead of almonds. Unbleached nuts make the macaroons darker in color, while blanched nuts give them a golden tone. Either way, the flavor is not affected.

Cover two baking sheets with kitchen parchment, or grease and flour lightly.

If the almonds are not already ground, grate in a blender or electric food processor. Mix the ground nuts with the sugar and egg whites in a heavy saucepan. Cook over moderate heat, stirring constantly, for 8 to 10 minutes or until the batter looks as thick as soft mashed potatoes. *Do not boil.* A good test is to pull a path through the batter with a spatula. When the path stays clear briefly, the batter is thick enough. Take off the heat and stir in the almond extract.

Drop from a teaspoon onto the prepared baking sheets. Let stand at room temperature for about one hour. Bake for 22 to 25 minutes. Once cooked, lift from the baking sheets immediately to a cake rack. Makes 2 dozen.

These macaroons keep perfectly if stored in an airtight container while still fresh.

Coconut

Follow directions for making Almond Macaroons, substituting 1 can (3½ ounces) flaked coconut for nuts. Stir in 3 tablespoons all-purpose flour with flavoring (½ teaspoon vanilla instead of almond extract).

Chocolate

Follow directions for making Almond Macaroons, substituting ½ cup semisweet chocolate pieces and 1½ cups grated or ground nuts for the almonds. Cook chocolate pieces with nuts, sugar and egg whites.

Candied Fruit Macaroons

Follow directions for making Almond Macaroons, substituting 1 cup chopped candied fruit (3½- and 4-ounce boxes of cherries, citron, pineapple, etc., are generally available) and 1 cup grated or ground nuts for the almonds. Cook candied fruits with nuts, sugar (½ cup instead of ¾ cup) and egg whites.

WALNUT CAKE

Shortening

1½ cups all-purpose flour

2 teaspoons baking powder

¼ teaspoon salt

½ cup (1 stick) butter or
    margarine

½ teaspoon vanilla

1 ⅓ cups sugar

2 tablespoons instant coffee
    dissolved in ½ cup boiling
    water

3 tablespoons boiling water

½ cup chopped walnuts

3 LEFTOVER EGG WHITES

Preheat oven to 350°.

Grease two 8-inch round cake pans and coat lightly with flour. Dump out any excess.

Combine the remaining flour, baking powder and salt in the sifter. Set aside.

Place the butter, vanilla and ½ cup of the sugar in the bowl of an electric mixer. Beat until very thick and creamy. Sift in the flour mixture alternately with the coffee. Place ⅓ cup of the sugar in a small saucepan over moderate heat until the sugar melts into a rich brown caramel syrup. Add 3 tablespoons boiling water and cook slowly for 10 minutes. Take off the heat. When caramel syrup is cooled but still running, add to flour mixture and then add walnuts.

Beat the egg whites with a rotary or electric beater until they form soft points. Gradually add the remaining ½ cup of sugar, beating hard. Continue beating until you have a satiny meringue that holds firm, shiny points.

Add the nut mixture to the meringue and fold in with a rubber spatula. Pour the batter into the prepared pans, dividing it evenly.

Bake for 20 to 25 minutes or until a toothpick comes out clean. Cook cake layers 10 minutes before turning onto racks.

Cool completely before frosting with Brown Sugar Frosting (page 128).

DATE AND WALNUT COOKIES

2 cups shelled walnuts,
    chopped fine
1½ cups (7¼-ounce package)
    dates, chopped fine

½ cup sugar
1 teaspoon vanilla
3 LEFTOVER EGG WHITES

Combine walnuts and dates. Then mix in the sugar and vanilla. Most easily done with your hands.

Beat the egg whites until they hold firm, shiny peaks when the beater is held straight up. Pick up about a third of the whites with a whip and mix thoroughly into the fruit mixture. Then pour over the whites and fold in gently with a rubber spatula.

Sprinkle granulated sugar over two baking sheets and drop the cookie batter by tablespoons. Then shape into peaks. Let stand overnight at room temperature. Bake the following day in a preheated 350° oven for 10 minutes. Cool 5 minutes before lifting from baking sheets. Makes 24.

SNOW BALLS

Butter or margarine
½ cup (1 stick) butter
1 cup sugar
2¼ cups all-purpose flour
3½ teaspoons baking powder

½ cup milk
Salt
Cream of tartar
4 LEFTOVER EGG WHITES

Preheat oven to 325°.

Butter 8 ramekins and set aside.

Work the butter until soft with a beater, gradually working in the sugar until light and creamy. Sift the flour and baking powder together. Beat into the butter mixture alternately with the milk. Add a good dash of salt and a big pinch of cream of tartar to the egg whites. Beat with an electric beater or in an electric mixer until they hold firm, shiny peaks when the beater is held straight up. Add about a third of the whites to the batter and beat in vigorously with a whip. Pour over the remaining whites and fold in gently with a rubber spatula. Spoon into the prepared ramekins. Place in a baking pan, add boiling water to reach to about three-fourths the depth of the ramekins and bake for 35 minutes. Serve with Lemon Sauce (page 218) to 8.

WELSH RABBIT, FRENCH STYLE

1 cup Sauce Béchamel
  (page 230)*
4 LEFTOVER EGG WHITES
¼ teaspoon cream of tartar
Salt

½ teaspoon baking powder
1½ cups grated Swiss cheese
  (about ¾ pound)
5 slices white bread, toasted
  lightly

Preheat oven to 400°.

Make the Béchamel and set it aside.

Beat the egg whites with the cream of tartar and a pinch of salt until they hold firm, shiny peaks when the beater is held straight up. Whip about one-third of the whites along with the baking powder into the Béchamel vigorously with a wire whip. Using a rubber spatula, gently fold in half the cheese and the remaining whites.

Press the toasted bread into five ramekins or custard cups, pushing it right down to the bottom. Fill with the cheese mixture and sprinkle each ramekin with some of the remaining cheese. Place on a baking sheet and bake for 20 to 25 minutes.

A perfect luncheon dish for 5, with, perhaps, a green salad and a glass of wine.

---

* Make the Sauce Béchamel in these proportions: 3 tablespoons butter or margarine; 3 tablespoons flour; 1 cup milk; season with salt, freshly ground white pepper and freshly grated nutmeg.

FISH LOAF

Butter or margarine
½ cup milk
3 slices firm bread,
   crumbled
1 pound boned, skinned fish
   (flounder, codfish, haddock)

5 LEFTOVER EGG WHITES
Salt
Freshly ground white pepper
1 cup Sauce Béchamel
   (page 230)*
Sauce Bercy (page 101)

Preheat oven to 425°.

Butter a 3-cup rectangular baking dish thoroughly and set aside.

Pour the milk into a bowl, add the crumbled bread and set it aside, too.

Cut the fish into small pieces. Purée half the fish and half the egg whites with a dash of salt and pepper in the container of a blender or electric food processor. Purée the remainder, then mix together. Refrigerate. Make the Sauce Béchamel, seal with plastic wrap to prevent a skin forming and refrigerate until cold. Meanwhile, work the bread and milk into a paste.

Once the fish purée and the Béchamel are cold, combine with the bread-milk paste. Season to taste with salt and pepper. Note: It takes a good bit of salt to bring up the full flavor of the fish.

Spoon the fish mixture into the prepared baking dish. Place a piece of waxed paper or kitchen parchment on top and bake for 50 to 60 minutes.

To serve, remove paper, unmold, slice and arrange on a heated platter. Serve with boiled potatoes and Sauce Bercy to 4 or 5.

---

* Make the Sauce Béchamel in these proportions: 3 tablespoons butter or margarine; 3 tablespoons flour; 1 cup milk. Season with salt and freshly ground white pepper.

CHEESE SOUFFLÉ AUX BLANCS

Butter or margarine
3 tablespoons finely grated
   Swiss cheese
1 cup Sauce Béchamel
   (page 230)*

6 LEFTOVER EGG WHITES
¼ teaspoon cream of tartar
1¼ cups coarsely grated Swiss
   cheese (about 4 ounces)

Preheat oven to 400°.

Take a 1-quart soufflé dish. Butter thoroughly, including the curve at the bottom, and coat with grated cheese. Dump out any excess and add to the other cheese. Refrigerate.

Beat the egg whites with the cream of tartar until they hold firm, shiny peaks when the beater is held straight up. Beat about a third of the whites into the Sauce Béchamel vigorously. Gently fold in the remaining whites and the cheese with a rubber spatula.

Pour into the prepared soufflé dish and place on a baking sheet in the oven. Bake for 25 to 30 minutes. In the event the top seems to be browning too much during baking, place a piece of foil lightly on top for the remainder of the cooking time. Serve at once.

BLUEBERRY SOUFFLÉ

Butter or margarine
1 cup sugar
2 cups blueberries, past
   their prime
Juice of ½ lemon, strained

3 tablespoons water
7 LEFTOVER EGG WHITES
Few drops almond extract
Grated rind of ½ lemon
¼ cup (scant) toasted, slivered
   almonds

* Make the Sauce Béchamel in these proportions: 3 tablespoons butter or margarine; 3 tablespoons flour; 1 cup milk; season with salt and freshly ground white pepper.

Preheat oven to 400°.

Butter a 1-quart soufflé dish. Coat with some of the sugar, dumping out any excess. Refrigerate.

Push the berries through a food mill or purée in an electric food processor. Sprinkle with the lemon juice.

Combine the remaining sugar and 3 tablespoons of water in a saucepan. Bring to a boil and cook until a candy thermometer reaches 280° or the syrup spins a thread when dripped from the tip of a spoon. Take off the heat and cool.

Beat the egg whites until they hold firm, shiny peaks when the beater is held straight up. Beat in the almond extract and the lemon rind.

Add sugar syrup to blueberries and then pour blueberry mixture over the whites and fold in gently with a rubber spatula. Pour into the prepared dish, place on a baking sheet and bake for 20 minutes. Sprinkle the almonds over the soufflé. Continue baking another 5 minutes. Serve immediately.

ANGEL CAKE

It may surprise you that I use all-purpose flour in my angel cake recipes, but after all these years of using cake flour (which is hard to get these days) I discovered that it doesn't matter one bit. You can make perfect, light and delicious angel cakes with all-purpose flour.

1¼ CUPS LEFTOVER EGG WHITES
  (8 TO 10)
¼ teaspoon salt
1 teaspoon cream of tartar

1½ cups sugar
1 teaspoon vanilla or
  ½ teaspoon almond extract
1 cup all-purpose flour

Preheat oven to 350°.

Place the egg whites, salt and cream of tartar in the bowl of an electric mixer. Beat at high speed until the whites just begin to hold a shape. Then begin to add the sugar in a slow, steady stream, beating hard and constantly. When all the sugar has been added, fold in the vanilla or almond extract.

Sift about ¼ cup of the flour at *one time* over the entire surface of the batter. Fold in with a rubber spatula. Take care not to overmix. Once all the flour has been incorporated, pour the batter into an ungreased 10-inch tube pan.

Bake for 35 to 40 minutes or until the cake springs back when pressed with your finger. Once baked, invert the pan over a wire cake rack and let it hang until completely cold. If the pan lacks "legs" place the tube over the neck of a funnel or bottle, so that the pan is suspended. When cold, loosen edges with a spatula. Give the pan a good bang and the cake will drop out.

To serve, pull the cake apart with two forks rather than cutting with a knife.

If you have an extra egg yolk and some strawberries on hand, finish the cake with Fresh Strawberry Glaze (page 219).

CHOCOLATE ANGEL CAKE

1 cup all-purpose flour
1½ cups sifted confectioners'
   sugar
¼ cup cocoa
1 tablespoon powdered
   instant coffee

1½ CUPS LEFTOVER EGG WHITES
   (ABOUT 10)
½ teaspoon salt
1½ teaspoons cream of tartar
1 cup granulated sugar

Preheat oven to 375°.

Sift flour, confectioners' sugar, cocoa and powdered instant coffee together 3 times. Set aside.

Place the egg whites in a very large mixing bowl or in the bowl of an electric mixer. Sprinkle with salt and cream of tartar. Beat the whites until they are frothy. At this point add the granulated sugar in a slow, steady stream, beating hard and constantly until they hold firm, shiny peaks.

Sift about ¼ cup of the flour mixture over the batter at one time. Using a rubber spatula, fold in until all patches of flour are incorporated into the batter. Do not overmix.

Pour into an ungreased 10-inch tube pan. Bake for 35 to 40 minutes or until the cake springs back when pressed with your finger. Take from the oven, invert over a wire rack and allow it to stand until completely cold. If the pan lacks "legs" place the tube over the neck of a funnel or bottle. When cold, loosen edges with a spatula, give the pan a bang and the cake will drop out. To serve, pull apart with two forks.

Egg on Your Face?

Believe it or not, egg whites make a marvelous beauty mask that will leave your face glowing for hours. Simply take some leftover egg white and spread it thinly over your face, avoiding eyes and lips. Allow it to dry, wash it off with warm water and see the difference!

Egg Yolks

CLASSIC MAYONNAISE

2 LEFTOVER EGG YOLKS
1 teaspoon prepared mustard
1 tablespoon tarragon or wine
  vinegar

Salt
Freshly ground white pepper
1½ cups peanut oil, vegetable
  oil or olive oil*

Place the egg yolks, mustard, vinegar, salt and pepper to taste in a mixing bowl. Beat vigorously for about a minute with a

* Or half peanut or vegetable and half olive oil.

wire whip. Then begin to add the oil slowly, almost drop by drop, whipping hard and constantly until all the oil is incorporated. In the event the finished mayonnaise seems too thick, beat in a little extra vinegar. Makes about 1½ cups.

BLENDER MAYONNAISE

2 LEFTOVER EGG YOLKS
½ teaspoon dry mustard
½ teaspoon salt

2 tablespoons vinegar or
  lemon juice
1 cup peanut oil, vegetable
  oil, or olive oil*

Place the egg yolks, mustard, salt, vinegar and ¼ cup of the oil in the container of an electric blender. Cover container and turn motor to high. Immediately remove the cover and quickly add remaining oil in a steady stream. When all the oil is added, turn off the motor instantly. Makes 1¼ cups.

To Salvage Curdled Mayonnaise

Place 1 tablespoon of the curdled mayonnaise in a warm dry bowl with 1 teaspoon prepared mustard. Whip with a wire whip until creamy. Add remaining mayonnaise, tablespoon by tablespoon, beating vigorously after each addition until creamy.

Salvaging Leftover Homemade Mayonnaise

It's a curious thing, but homemade mayonnaise stored in the refrigerator—no matter how carefully covered—will thin down when brought to room temperature. It is, essentially, curdled. However, it can be salvaged, just as you would any curdled mayonnaise.

* Or half peanut or vegetable and half olive oil.

TURKISH SAUCE

A fascinating sauce from the other side of the world to serve with hard-cooked eggs or cold poached fish.

1 cup fresh bread crumbs

3 LEFTOVER EGG YOLKS, LIGHTLY BEATEN

1 small clove garlic, crushed, peeled and minced

1½ cups olive oil or vegetable oil or half and half

Juice of ½ lemon, strained, or to taste

Salt

Freshly ground pepper

Mix the crumbs, egg yolks and garlic together well. Beat in the oil and lemon juice. Add salt and pepper to taste. Makes about 1⅔ cups.

ONION BUTTER

½ cup (1 stick) butter or margarine

2 tablespoons finely chopped onion

3 LEFTOVER EGG YOLKS

Juice of ½ lemon

Salt

Dash cayenne pepper

4 to 5 sprigs parsley, minced

Place the butter, onion and ½ cup water in a saucepan. Bring to a boil and cook until all the water has boiled away and the onion is tender. With a wire whip beat together the egg yolks, lemon juice, salt and cayenne to taste. Add hot onion and parsley, mixing well. Makes about ⅔ cup. Serve hot over cooked vegetables.

ZABAGLIONE

4 LEFTOVER EGG YOLKS

Dash of brandy, if you're

¼ *cup sugar*

feeling expansive

½ *cup Marsala or dry sherry*

Combine the yolks and sugar in a heavy saucepan and beat with an electric egg beater until pale yellow and creamy. Pour into the top of the double boiler and place *over* simmering water (not boiling). Note the word "over." The bottom of the top half of the double boiler should not be in the water.

Beat in the wine (and brandy) and cook, beating constantly with a wire whip, until the mixture begins to foam and swells into a light, soft mass. At this point it is ready to serve.

Spoon into sherbet or wine or champagne glasses and serve immediately. Serves about 6.

ZUPPA PAVESE

A charming first course from Italy. Golden egg yolks floating on a toast raft.

Butter or margarine

4 cups meat (page 10) or

4 slices Italian or French

poultry (page 59) broth

bread

4 LEFTOVER EGG YOLKS

Freshly grated Parmesan

cheese

Preheat oven to 350°.

Butter one side of each slice of bread generously. Place, buttered side up, on a baking sheet. Bake 15 to 20 minutes or until toasted and crusty. Sprinkle each slice with 1 tablespoon of the cheese and slide under the broiler just long enough to brown the cheese lightly.

Meanwhile, heat the broth to the boiling point and ladle into 4 heated soup bowls or plates. Float a slice of the hot toast in each and allow it to stand just long enough for the edges to curl up slightly (2 or 3 minutes). Then, with care, slip a raw egg yolk on top of the toast in each bowl. Pass more cheese if you like.

SOUR CREAM COOKIES

1 cup (2 sticks) butter or
   margarine
2 cups sugar
4 LEFTOVER EGG YOLKS
1 teaspoon almond extract
1 cup commercial sour
   cream

5½ cups all-purpose flour
1 teaspoon baking soda
3 teaspoons baking powder
½ teaspoon salt
1 teaspoon ground coriander

Preheat oven to 400°.

Combine the butter and sugar in the big bowl of an electric mixer and beat until the mixture makes ribbons. Add the egg yolks and almond extract and continue beating until light and creamy. Stir in the sour cream. Combine the flour, baking soda, baking powder, salt and coriander in the sifter. Sift over the batter. Stir in or mix in with the beater. Cover and refrigerate until firm.

On a lightly floured board or pastry cloth, roll the dough out about ⅛ inch thick. Cut with a 2-inch cookie cutter or cut into 2-inch squares. Place on a baking sheet leaving a little space between. Bake for 8 to 10 minutes or until golden. Makes about 10 dozen.

PAVÉ AU CHOCOLAT

4 squares (1-ounce size)
  unsweetened chocolate
½ cup (1 stick) butter or
  margarine, cut into pieces
¾ cup sifted confectioners'
  sugar
4 LEFTOVER EGG YOLKS

2 tablespoons kirsch or dark
  rum
½ cup water
2 packages (3-ounce size)
  ladyfingers
Shelled pistachio nuts,
  chopped fine (optional)

Melt the chocolate over simmering water in the top of a double boiler.

Combine the butter and sugar in a bowl and beat with a rotary or electric beater until creamy. Add the egg yolks, one at a time, beating hard after each addition. Finally, stir in the melted chocolate.

Combine the kirsch or rum with the water in a flat shallow pan. Take a third of the ladyfingers and dip into this mixture quickly (don't allow them to soak or they'll break apart) and place in a row on an oblong serving platter. Coat the top with the chocolate. Then build up two more layers of the fingers with the chocolate filling between.

Frost the sides, then the top of the *pavé*. Shower the top with nuts. Refrigerate for at least 3 hours to allow the *pavé* to mellow. Serves 6 to 8.

CRÈME ANGLAISE
(*English Cream*)

A pouring custard, this might well be called all-purpose since it has so many uses: as a sauce with fresh or poached fruits, molded creams, puddings and dessert soufflés, and as a substitute for fresh cream. It is also a delicious dessert on its own.

½ cup sugar

4 LEFTOVER EGG YOLKS

1 teaspoon cornstarch

1¾ cups milk

2 teaspoons vanilla or almond extract

Beat the sugar into the egg yolks and continue beating until the mixture is very thick, and creamy, pale yellow in color, and makes ribbons when it falls back on itself. This is best done with an electric beater or mixer. Beat in the cornstarch. Heat the milk until a film shines on top—don't boil it. While beating constantly, add the hot milk to the yolk mixture, pouring in a thin, steady stream. Place over very low heat and cook, stirring constantly with a wooden spatula, until the sauce thickens just enough to coat a metal spoon (sauce should never come to a simmer). Take off the heat, beat for a minute or two to cool, then beat in the flavoring. Makes about 2½ cups.

BOILED DRESSING

This is the sauce America used before the "discovery" of mayonnaise—primarily for potato salad and cole slaw.

1½ teaspoons salt

1 teaspoon dry mustard

1 tablespoon sugar

4 LEFTOVER EGG YOLKS

1½ cups milk

½ cup vinegar

4 tablespoons (½ stick) butter or margarine

Mix dry ingredients. Beat the egg yolks well, stir in dry ingredients, next the milk, then slowly add the vinegar. Place in the top of a double boiler with the butter and cook over simmering water, stirring constantly, until sauce thickens. Cool.

CLASSIC HOLLANDAISE SAUCE

3 sticks (1½ cups) sweet
   butter
4 LEFTOVER EGG YOLKS
Salt

Freshly ground white pepper
Cayenne pepper
1 tablespoon lemon juice,
   strained

Heat the butter to the bubbling point but do not let it brown. Place the egg yolks in the top of a double boiler (not aluminum) and beat for 1 minute with a whip, then place over simmering water. Using a wire whip, beat vigorously for 8 to 10 minutes or until the mixture is thick and creamy. Take care not to curdle the eggs but if that happens, see below. When perfectly combined you can see the bottom of the pan between strokes and the mixture will never be so hot you can't dip your finger into it.

Take off the heat, place the pan on a damp cloth to keep it from turning as you beat. Add the hot butter in dribbles, beating constantly. When all the butter has been added, season with salt, pepper and cayenne to taste. Finally, stir in the lemon juice. Keep warm in a pan of tepid water, not hot or your sauce will separate. Hollandaise is always served lukewarm or tepid. Makes 2 cups.

Leftover Hollandaise can be refrigerated successfully for a few days (sealed with plastic wrap) or frozen. To heat, place in a pan of tepid water until the right temperature has been reached; to thaw, bring out of the freezer a couple of hours before using, then heat as directed.

To salvage Hollandaise (either classic or blender): If your sauce has not thickened or has curdled place 1 teaspoon of lemon juice and 1 tablespoon of the sauce in a bowl that has been rinsed in hot water then dried. Beat with a wire whip until the mixture becomes creamy and thickens. Then beat in the remainder of the sauce, about 1 tablespoon at a time, beating vigorously until it is creamy before adding the next tablespoon.

BLENDER HOLLANDAISE

¾ cup (1½ sticks) butter   *¼ teaspoon salt*
3 LEFTOVER EGG YOLKS   *Freshly ground white pepper*
2 tablespoons lemon juice   *Pinch cayenne pepper*

Heat the butter to the bubbling point but do not let it brown. Place the yolks, lemon juice, salt, pepper and cayenne in the container of the blender. Cover and turn motor high. Immediately remove the cover and quickly pour in the hot butter in a thin, steady stream. Once the butter has been added, turn off the motor immediately.

You can keep the Hollandaise warm by setting the container in a saucepan with about 2 inches of warm (*not hot*) water. Makes ¾ cup.

For a slightly larger quantity, use 4 egg yolks and 1 cup (2 sticks) of butter.

DONA HELMA'S PAPO DE ANJO
(*Angel's Double Chin*)

Dona Helma's Casa Brazil is one of New York's most splendid restaurants.

Butter or margarine   *2 cups water*
12 LEFTOVER EGG YOLKS   *20 whole cloves*
3 cups sugar

Preheat oven to 375°.

Butter 12 custard cups or ramekins thoroughly.

Beat the egg yolks with an electric beater or in an electric mixer until they triple in bulk and are very thick and creamy. Measure exactly ¼ cup of the beaten yolks into each buttered cup. Place the cups on a baking sheet and bake for 10 minutes.

Meanwhile, combine the sugar, water and 8 of the cloves in a large wide skillet. Stir until the sugar has dissolved and the mixture comes to a boil. Reduce the heat and boil slowly for 2 to 3 minutes. Turn six of the baked yolks into the bubbling syrup and poach, basting constantly, for 2 minutes. Lift from the pan to a flat dish. Poach the remaining yolks the same way.

Stick a clove into each angel and strain the syrup over all. Refrigerate, covered with plastic wrap or foil, for several hours or overnight. Serve cold, two to a person with a spoonful of the perfumed syrup.

Hard-cooked Eggs

HOW TO MAKE THE MOST OF LEFTOVER HARD-COOKED EGGS

Egg Sauce

1 cup medium Sauce Béchamel (page 230) and 2 or 3 hard-cooked eggs. Chop the whites and stir into the sauce. Force the yolks through a sieve and sprinkle over the sauce when served. Serve with chicken or fish.

Egg Sandwiches

Chop hard-cooked eggs or mash cooked yolks. Season with salt and paprika and mix in enough mayonnaise or Mustard Sauce (page 231) to hold the eggs together. Add, if you like, any of the following: chopped olives, green peppers, pimiento, pickle, cucumber, celery, cress, parsley and a seasoning of Worcestershire or Tabasco sauce.

Or you can add anchovy paste to the mashed yolks or chopped eggs.

Another variation is to add grated cheese and prepared mustard to chopped eggs and mix with mayonnaise.

Potato Salad

Peel and dice cooked potatoes. Add hard-cooked eggs, quartered or sliced, chopped celery, chopped green pepper, minced onions and chopped parsley. Mix well and add enough mayonnaise or Boiled Dressing (page 145) to hold the salad together.

Hard-cooked Egg Salad

Chop 5 hard-cooked eggs. Mix with ¼ cup mayonnaise or Boiled Dressing (page 145) seasoned with Worcestershire, mustard, salt and pepper. Serve in lettuce leaves with a garnish of chopped pimiento.

Stuffed Eggs

Peel hard-cooked eggs, cut in half, remove yolks and mash. Combine mashed yolks with ground ham or any leftover fish, shellfish or meat. Season and mix with enough Sauce Vinaigrette (page 229) to hold the mixture together. Refill whites and serve on lettuce leaves with more Sauce Vinaigrette on the side.

Beet and Egg Salad

Combine sliced cooked beets and hard-cooked eggs in a bowl. Add a little chopped onion or chives. Mix with Sauce Vinaigrette (page 229) and serve on lettuce or watercress.

Omelets

Were Omelets Made to Accommodate Leftovers?

Whoever made the first omelet (French, Italian or Spanish—they all claim it) certainly had an eye for value received and a profound respect for leftovers. As a meal in itself the omelet is superb, but as a carrier for leftover vegetables, fish, meat, even bread it has no equal. Herewith, the basic omelet recipe and some omelet fillings.

BASIC OMELET FOR ONE PERSON*

3 eggs
1 tablespoon cold water
Freshly ground pepper

¼ teaspoon salt, scant
1 tablespoon lightly salted
butter

Beat the eggs with a rotary beater or whip until they begin to foam. Do not overbeat or the eggs will become liquid, like water. Properly beaten they look stringy and make threads when you lift up the beater or whip. Heat the omelet pan over medium heat until hot. To test, flick a few drops of water on the pan. If it jumps around, your pan is ready. If steam rises the pan is too hot—in which case, take it off the heat and wave in the air to cool it down. Add butter (*if it's a new pan*, butter the sides all the way up to the top).

* Adapted from *Omelets, Crêpes and Other Recipes* by Rudolph Stanish, the Omelet King.

Pour the eggs into the hot pan. Then with the flat side of a fork, make circular motions around the bottom of the pan *fast*, as you would making scrambled eggs. Speed is of the essence for lightness and fluffiness. While the right hand is making circular motions, shake the pan with the left hand, rocking it back and forth, to keep the eggs loose. When the eggs are cooked and all the liquid is firm, spread the eggs evenly but lightly with a fork to cover any breaks in the surface. Pause briefly to allow the eggs to set. (If you are going to use a filling this is the time to place it on the egg.)

To turn the omelet out, grasp the handle of the pan with your left hand, *palm side up* (this makes it easier to tilt and finally roll the omelet out). Now tilt the pan at a 45° angle, and with the fork in your right hand, as close as possible to the handle, begin to roll the omelet away from the handle to the opposite edge of the pan and onto a heated plate.

The perfect omelet is firm on the outside, pure egg color without brown, and fluffy and soufflé-like on the inside. With practice, any cook can, and should, do the entire operation in 1 minute flat. The omelet should be served at once.

FILLINGS FOR OMELETS

Chicken Liver Garnish

Sauté a few sliced chicken livers in butter or margarine over a high heat until lightly colored all over, about 1 minute. Heat a tablespoon or so of dry sherry, ignite and pour over the livers. Sprinkle with a pinch of arrowroot. Stir into the liquid to thicken lightly. Keep warm.

Once the omelet is on the serving plate, make a slit down the middle and spoon the liver garnish into the opening. Serve with watercress.

Mushroom

Sauté 3 minced mushrooms in 1 tablespoon peanut or vegetable oil. Sprinkle with salt and continue cooking until all the liquid has evaporated. Make a basic omelet and add the mushrooms to the eggs.

Rice

Place 3 eggs in a bowl. Add ½ cup cooked rice, ½ teaspoon salt and ¼ teaspoon Tabasco. Beat with a fork until just mixed. Butter the omelet pan and add the egg mixture, following directions for basic omelet.

Spinach

Beat 2 or 3 tablespoons of cooked spinach purée into the eggs. Then follow directions for basic omelet.

Potatoes and Minced Herbs

Sauté ¼ cup cooked potatoes, mix with some minced herbs and sprinkle over the omelet when the eggs are set.

Ham

Take ¼ cup diced cooked ham and sprinkle over the omelet when the eggs are set.

Shrimp, Crab or Lobster

Sauté ¼ cup diced shrimp, crab or lobster and sprinkle over the omelet when the eggs are set.

Stale White Bread

Sauté ¼ cup cubed stale white bread in butter or margarine and sprinkle over the omelet when the eggs are set.

FRITTATA
(Open-faced Italian Omelet)

The *frittata* given here is the basic technique and the fillings
that can be used are limited only by the cook's imagination.

6 eggs

¼ teaspoon salt

Freshly ground pepper to taste

1 cup freshly grated Parmesan
or Swiss cheese (4 ounces)

3 tablespoons butter or
margarine

Combine the eggs, salt and pepper in a bowl and beat until well
mixed. Then beat in the cheese. Melt the butter in a 12-inch
skillet over medium heat. When the butter froths (take care
not to let it brown), add the eggs and reduce heat to the
lowest possible point.

Once the eggs have set but the top is still runny, cook the
frittata 15 minutes longer. Traditionally the *frittata* is turned to
cook on the other side, (experts flip it over in midair), but you
will probably find it easier to run it under the broiler for about
half a minute or so. Neither the top nor bottom should be
browned. Properly cooked, a *frittata* is set but still soft.

To serve, loosen the *frittata* with a spatula and transfer
to a warm platter. Serve in wedges.

With *asparagus*. Cut the cooked asparagus into ½-inch lengths.
Mix into the *frittata* at the same time you add the cheese.

With *green beans*. Chop the cold cooked beans coarsely and
mix into the *frittata* along with the cheese.

With *cooked ham*. Chop the ham coarsely and mix into the
frittata along with the cheese.

With zucchini. Chop the cold cooked zucchini and mix into the *frittata* along with the cheese and a few sprigs of parsley or basil leaves, minced.

With spinach. Squeeze the cold cooked spinach dry, then chop fairly fine. Mix into the *frittata* when you mix in the cheese.

VEGETABLES, HERBS, GREENS

Buying and Storing Fresh Vegetables

If you buy a week's supply of vegetables at one time, as many of us do, here is a general guide from the U. S. Department of Agriculture. Remember, the fresher the vegetable the better it is when eaten.

Don't wash fruits and vegetables until just before using. If they are wet or damp while under refrigeration they will mold and/or rot.

One of the best pieces of equipment available is the lettuce dryer, which makes it possible to wash and dry instantly any leafy greens. The dryer is available in stores specializing in fine cooking equipment and in most stores which sell housewares.

Asparagus
Do not wash before storing. Refrigerate in the crisper, plastic bags or plastic containers.
    Use within 2 to 3 days.

Broccoli and Brussels Sprouts
Refrigerate in crisper, plastic bags or plastic containers.
    Use within 3 to 5 days.

Cabbage, Cauliflower, Celery and Snap Beans
Refrigerate in crisper, plastic bags or plastic containers.

Use cabbage within 1 or 2 weeks; cauliflower, celery and beans within 1 week.

To freeze celery tops and leaves and outer ribs, chop off the leaves and tops, place in a freezer bag, squeeze out all air, tie securely and freeze. Use in making soups, stock, stews, etc., in fact, in any recipe calling for celery.

Carrots, Beets, Parsnips, Radishes and White Turnips

Cut off tops. Refrigerate in plastic bags or plastic containers.

Use within 2 weeks.

If your luck with carrots, and I mean the carrots that come in bags, is like mine they will show what sometimes seems to be instantaneous signs of age. When this happens, peel them and cut them so they will fit into a Mason jar. Fill with cold water. Cover and refrigerate.

When you use them, don't throw the water away—use it in making broths.

Green Peas and Limas

Refrigerate in pods in crisper.

Use within 3 to 5 days.

Lettuce and Other Salad Greens

When you get the lettuce home, strip off any leaves that seem too coarse for salad and freeze them for later use. Place in a plastic bag, squeeze out all air and tie securely. Refrigerate.

Use within a week.

Onions

Store mature onions at room temperature or slightly cooler, in loosely woven or open-mesh containers. Stored this way, they keep several months. At high temperature and high humidity, however, they sprout and decay. Keep green onions (or scallions) cold and moist in the refrigerator, stored in plastic bags.

Use within 3 to 5 days.

Parsley

I keep my fresh parsley refrigerated in a big Mason jar with a tight cover. When I get it home from the market I run it under cold water and shake off any excess. Then I look it over very carefully and discard immediately any damaged or discolored stalks, putting the remainder in the Mason jar. Whenever I use any, I discard those with yellowed leaves. A tip on parsley— save the parsley stalks and add to soups or broth.

Note: Parsley loses its flavor if frozen.

Peppers and Cucumbers

Refrigerate in crisper or in plastic bags.

Use within 1 week.

Potatoes

Store in a dark, dry place with good ventilation away from any source of heat, with a cool temperature of about 45° to 50°. Potatoes stored this way will keep several months. Light causes greening, which makes the potatoes taste bitter. High temperatures hasten sprouting and shriveling.

If stored at room temperature, use within a week.

Rhubarb

A vegetable that is often used as a fruit, it is ready to use when purchased. Refrigerate in crisper or in plastic bags.

Use within 3 to 5 days.

Spinach, Kale, Collards, Chard, Beet Greens, Turnip and Mustard Greens

Wash thoroughly in cold water. Lift (do not drain) from the water so that any grit will settle in the bottom of the pan. Drain thoroughly. Refrigerate in crisper or in plastic bags.

Use within 3 to 5 days.

Summer Squashes—Yellow or Green

Refrigerate in crisper, plastic bags or plastic containers.

Use within 3 to 5 days.

Sweet Corn
Refrigerate, unhusked and uncovered.
For sweetest flavor use as soon as possible.

Sweet Potatoes, Hard-rind Squashes, Eggplant and
Rutabagas (Yellow Turnips)
Stored at cool room temperature (around 60°), they will keep
several months.
If stored at room temperature, use within a week.

Tomatoes
Refrigerate uncovered. Depending on ripeness, they will keep
up to a week. To ripen unripe tomatoes, place in a plastic bag
with a very ripe apple, punch a few holes in the bag.
The ripe apple (like all fruit) gives off ethylene gas which
stimulates unripe fruit to ripen. Since fruit breathes, taking
in oxygen and giving off carbon dioxide, the punched holes
allow the excess carbon dioxide to escape. True, some of the
ethylene gas also escapes but enough remains to speed up the
ripening of the tomatoes.
A temperature of 65° to 75° is best for ripening. Below
65°, ripening is retarded. Hence, place them in the refrigerator
when slow ripening is your objective. Once ripe, if not eaten
immediately, tomatoes and other fruits should be refrigerated.
Bring to room temperature, however, before using.

Watercress
Do not wash. Fill a glass with cold water. Place the watercress
in the glass, cover with a plastic bag and secure with a rubber
band. With its feet in water your cress will survive for as much
as a week depending, of course, on its freshness when you
bought it.

CURRIED VEGETABLES

4 tablespoons (½ stick) butter
  or margarine
1 small yellow onion, peeled
  and chopped
1 teaspoon curry powder
½ teaspoon salt

1 tablespoon cornstarch or
  arrowroot
1 cup vegetable liquor or
  water
2 CUPS LEFTOVER VEGETABLES
  (PEAS, CARROTS, LIMA BEANS)

Melt the butter in a saucepan. Add the onion and sauté until lightly browned. Mix the curry powder, salt and cornstarch together. Stir into the onions until smooth. Add the vegetable liquor slowly, stirring constantly. Cook over low heat until the sauce has thickened, then add vegetables. Serve with cold roast lamb to 4.

CREAM OF LEFTOVER
VEGETABLE SOUP

Here is a tasty soup that will use up your leftover vegetables—a bit of cooked potato and two or three other items, such as spinach, carrots, cauliflower, Brussels sprouts, celery, peas, or whatever you have on hand.

1 small yellow onion, peeled
  and minced
3 tablespoons butter or
  margarine
½ cup water
½ cup cooked potatoes
1½ cups poultry broth
  (page 59)

½ teaspoon celery salt
Salt
Freshly ground white pepper
1 CUP LEFTOVER VEGETABLES
1 cup light cream or milk
Minced parsley, chives or
  celery leaves

Combine the onion, butter and ½ cup of water in a saucepan. Bring to a boil, then simmer until all the water has boiled away and the onion is tender. Stir in the potatoes, the broth, seasonings and vegetables. Bring to a boil. Simmer for 5 to 10 minutes. Push through a food mill or purée in an electric blender. Pour back into the saucepan and stir in the cream, adding salt and pepper to taste.

Serve hot or cold with one of the garnishes to 4 or 5 people.

VEGETABLE SOUFFLÉ

Cooked spinach, carrots, cauliflower, broccoli, asparagus, mushrooms, cut green beans, peas or lima beans are all good bases for this soufflé.

8 *tablespoons (1 stick) butter*
  or margarine
2 *tablespoons dry bread*
  crumbs
⅔ *cup all-purpose flour*
1 *cup milk, heated*
1 *cup chicken broth, heated*
2 *tablespoons grated Swiss or*
  Parmesan cheese

4 *whole eggs, separated*
¾ CUP LEFTOVER CHOPPED
  VEGETABLES
Salt
Freshly ground pepper
2 *extra egg whites*
Cream of tartar

Preheat oven to 375°.

Butter a 2-quart soufflé mold thoroughly, including the curve at the bottom. Coat with bread crumbs, dumping out any excess. Refrigerate.

Heat the remaining butter in a heavy saucepan. Stir in the flour and cook over low heat, stirring constantly, until the mixture froths, about 5 minutes. Add the milk and broth. Beat briskly with a wire whip until the sauce thickens. Continue to cook, whipping constantly until smooth. Stir in the cheese. Take off the heat and cool slightly.

Add the yolks, one at a time, beating hard after each addition. Stir in the vegetables. Add salt and pepper to taste. Soufflé can be prepared to this point in advance, in which case, seal the surface with plastic wrap.

Beat the egg whites with a dash of cream of tartar and salt until they hold firm, shiny peaks when the beater is held straight up. Beat about a third into the vegetable mixture with a wire whip. Pour the mixture over the remaining whites and fold in gently with a rubber spatula. Pour into the prepared mold.

Place on a baking sheet and bake for 35 to 40 minutes. For a firm, rather than a creamy center, bake another 5 to 10 minutes. Serve at once.

"PIQUANTE" BEETS

2 or 3 LEFTOVER BEETS
2 tablespoons wine vinegar
1 teaspoon salt
1 tablespoon sugar
Freshly ground pepper
1 tablespoon butter

Mince the beets. Place in a saucepan with vinegar and seasonings over low heat until piping hot, stirring constantly. Add the butter. Very good, hot or cold, with beef or lamb.

BEETS IN ORANGE SAUCE

These are especially good with roast pork or pork chops.

1 cup orange juice
1½ teaspoons brown sugar
Dash salt
Several twists of the peppermill
1 teaspoon cornstarch
1 tablespoon butter or margarine
1 CUP SLICED LEFTOVER BEETS

Combine all the ingredients except the beets in a heavy sauce-pan. Bring to a boil, stirring constantly until you have a smooth sauce. Add the beets, bring up to a boil, and serve to 3 or 4.

Hang on to the Beet Tops

If by some miracle you get fresh young beets with tops on, you're in for a surprise. Use the beets for one meal and save the tops for another. Wash thoroughly. Place in a heavy sauce-pan with all the water clinging to them. Sprinkle with a bit of salt and cook, *uncovered*, until the greens are thoroughly wilted and tender. Drain well, season with salt, freshly ground pepper and lots of butter.

Tops from two pounds of beets will serve about 4.

CARROT RING

3 tablespoons butter or margarine
5 or 6 LEFTOVER COOKED CARROTS, PURÉED
1 cup milk

Salt
Freshly ground pepper
Sugar
4 egg yolks, well beaten

Preheat oven to 350°.

Butter a 9-inch ring mold. Mix the remaining butter with all other ingredients, adding salt, pepper and sugar to taste. Pour into the prepared mold. Place in a baking pan. Add enough very hot water from the tap to reach to two-thirds the depth of the mold. Bake for 30 to 40 minutes or until firm.

To serve, turn out on a heated platter and fill the center with any creamed vegetable or meat. Serves 4 or 5.

CAULIFLOWER SOUP

1 to 1½ CUPS LEFTOVER
 CAULIFLOWER
3 cups chicken broth
4 tablespoons (½ stick)
 butter or margarine

1 yellow onion, peeled and
 chopped fine
Salt
Freshly ground white pepper
Grated cheese
Rye toast

Purée the cauliflower, a small amount at a time, with some of the broth in an electric blender. Melt the butter in a heavy saucepan. Add the onion and sauté over moderate heat, stirring occasionally, until the onion is golden. Add the cauliflower purée and all remaining broth. Bring to a boil. Season with salt and pepper to taste.

Serve piping hot with a sprinkling of cheese accompanied by toasted cocktail rye bread. Delicious. Serves about 4.

CELERY SOUP

This is a practical way to make the most of the outside ribs of a bunch of celery, which always seem to deteriorate faster than you can use them up.

5 or 6 OUTER RIBS OF CELERY
1 large piece of lemon rind
 (page 216)
1 cup water
1 teaspoon salt
2 tablespoons vegetable,
 peanut or olive oil
5 to 10 sprigs parsley, minced

1 or 2 cloves garlic, crushed
 and peeled
¼ cup tomato purée
3 cups poultry (page 59) or
 meat (page 10) broth
Grated cheese, Parmesan or
 Swiss

Wash the celery ribs, then chop coarsely. Place in a heavy kettle with the lemon rind, water and salt. Bring to a boil, reduce heat to a simmer, cover and cook slowly until tender to the bite.

Heat the oil in a small saucepan. Add the parsley and garlic. Sauté for a couple of minutes over low heat. Add the tomato purée, cover and simmer 10 minutes. When the celery has cooked, add the tomato mixture and the broth. Let the soup mellow for a full day or overnight, or it can be frozen to serve later.

Before serving, bring to a boil, then simmer for about 30 minutes.

Serve piping hot in heated soup plates with a garnish of cheese. Serves about 4.

How to Make the Most of a Bunch of Celery

Keep a sharp eye on the celery in your refrigerator and make the most of it before it goes down the drain.

Add the fresh tops, chopped, to salads, or freeze (page 158) and add to the pot when you're making soups.

Stuff the ribs with a mixture of softened cream cheese and Roquefort cheese, seasoned with Worcestershire sauce; or with softened cream cheese mixed with chopped stuffed olives, or chopped ripe olives, or crumbled crisp bacon, or minced pimientos or what have you. Softened sharp cheese (Gorgonzola, for example) mixed with some minced fresh parsley is also a delicious stuffing. Once stuffed, refrigerate the ribs until they are well chilled.

CREAM OF CORN SOUP

3 LEFTOVER EARS CORN ON THE
   COB OR ¾ CUP LEFTOVER
   WHOLE KERNEL CORN
1 *tablespoon butter or*
   margarine
½ *small yellow onion, peeled*
   and minced

½ *cup water*
1 *tablespoon all-purpose flour*
1 *cup milk*
Salt
Freshly ground pepper
Freshly grated nutmeg
Minced parsley or chives

To take the corn off the cob without skins, first score each cob
down its full length with the tines of a fork. Then, with the
back of a knife, scrape the corn "meat" off the cob onto a piece
of waxed paper or a plate.

     Heat the butter in a medium saucepan. Add the onion and
the water. Bring to a boil and continue boiling until the water
has all evaporated and the onion is tender. Sprinkle with the
flour and cook, stirring, 2 to 3 minutes. Add the corn, milk,
salt, pepper and nutmeg to taste. Bring up to a boil and simmer
for about 5 minutes. Makes 3 to 4 cups. Garnish with the
parsley or chives before serving.

CORN GALETTES

3 LEFTOVER EARS COOKED CORN
   OR ¾ CUP WHOLE KERNEL
   CORN
1 *egg*
¼ *cup milk*

3 *tablespoons all-purpose*
   flour
Salt
Freshly ground black pepper
Oil for frying

Strip the "meat" off corn like this: Pull the tines of a fork
down each ear all around to break the skin. Then with the back
of a strong knife scrape each ear onto waxed paper or a plate.

     Beat egg with milk, flour, and salt and pepper to taste.

Combine with the corn and shape into small flat cakes. Heat a little oil in a skillet, and sauté the cakes on both sides until golden. Makes 4 to 5 cakes.

LETTUCE SOUP

OUTER LEAVES OF LETTUCE, ESCAROLE OR CHICORY (ABOUT 2 CUPS)
3 cups milk
2 tablespoons butter or margarine
1 yellow onion, peeled and minced
½ cup water
2 tablespoons all-purpose flour
Salt
Freshly ground white pepper

Wash the leaves and cut away any brown or bruised parts. Chop coarsely. Place in a blender or electric food processor with 1 cup of the milk. Purée at high speed.

Melt the butter in a skillet. Add the onion and water. Bring to a boil and cook until all the water has boiled away and the onion is soft and transparent. Stir in the flour and cook over moderate heat until the mixture froths, about 3 minutes. Stir in the lettuce and milk mixture and the remaining milk. Bring to a boil, stirring constantly. Season to taste with salt and pepper. Makes about 3 cups.

Variations: Substitute yoghurt or sour cream for some of the milk; add cottage cheese or softened cream cheese when you purée the greens—in this case, do not add flour.

Freeze the Outside Leaves of Lettuce

Often the outside leaves of a head of lettuce are bruised and discolored. Wash and dry well, place in a freezer bag, squeeze out all air, tie securely and freeze. Use in making soups along with leftover lettuce.

How to Make the Most of the Outer Leaves of Iceberg Lettuce

Add to the saucepan when cooking peas, green beans or carrots to increase flavor and vitamin content.

Use as a lid to keep leftover casseroles moist when reheating them in the oven.

To heat rolls or buns and keep them moist, cover with lettuce leaves, then wrap in foil and warm in a moderate oven.

Spread leaves with cottage cheese or yoghurt mixed with any of the following: chopped fruit, diced cooked vegetables, flaked cooked fish, or chunks of cooked chicken or turkey. Roll up like a jelly roll and eat out of hand.

CHARLOTTE MAYERSON'S SOUPE DE SALADE

If you have a cup or so of leftover salad, including the dressing, you can turn it into a delicious, piquant soup. To it you can add any leftover raw or cooked vegetables (I have even added those drained from a marinade) such as tomatoes, cucumbers, etc.

2 to 3 tablespoons oil
1 CUP OR MORE LEFTOVER
   SALAD WITH THE DRESSING
Any available leftover
   vegetables
Leftover lettuce leaves

Chicken broth, or chicken
   cubes or instant bouillon*
Salt
Freshly ground pepper
Heavy cream or sour cream
   (optional)

* The amount of broth depends on the amount of salad. Allow about 1 cup to 1 cup of salad, more or less. Obviously, if you use cubes or instant bouillon you follow package directions to make the broth.

Heat 2 or 3 tablespoons of oil in a heavy saucepan. Add the salad and whatever else you have to the pan. Sauté over a fairly good heat for 5 to 10 minutes, stirring occasionally. Pour into the container of an electric blender with some of the chicken broth and purée at high speed. Combine with any remaining broth in a saucepan and bring to a boil. If you like, add some heavy cream or sour cream. Taste for seasoning. Chances are you won't need any.

WHITE MUSHROOM SAUCE

Let's say you have a few mushrooms that are beginning to show their age. You can turn them into a very nice sauce, indeed, to serve with eggs, vegetables or poultry. Or just to top a nice crisp piece of buttered toast.

5 or 6 LARGE MUSHROOMS, WITH STEMS, COARSELY CHOPPED

4 tablespoons butter or margarine

Lemon juice to taste

1½ tablespoons all-purpose flour

1 generous cup milk or half and half

Freshly grated nutmeg

Salt

Freshly ground pepper

Sauté the mushrooms in 2 tablespoons of the butter for 3 or 4 minutes. Then stir in the lemon juice. Scrape out of the pan onto waxed paper or foil.

Melt the remaining butter in the pan. Stir in the flour until smooth. Cook, stirring, over moderate heat for 3 to 4 minutes. Add the milk. Cook, beating constantly with a whip until the sauce is smooth and has a light consistency. Stir in the mushrooms and pan drippings. Season to taste with nutmeg, salt and pepper. Bring up to a boil if it is to be served immediately. Otherwise, cover with plastic wrap so a skin won't form. Makes about 1½ cups.

DUXELLES MADE WITH
MUSHROOM STEMS

Duxelles, a mixture of raw mushrooms, green onion bulbs, onions, parsley and seasonings, is used to stuff large mushroom caps and such vegetables as onions or tomatoes; with or without bread crumbs to stuff chicken or game; combined with Sauce Béchamel (page 230) to make meat or potato croquettes. It is also used as a foundation for various sauces, or can be turned into a sauce by the simple addition of cream and/or wine and served with meat.

To make duxelles with mushroom stems only, chop the stems very, very fine. Place in a fresh towel and twist to extract as much juice as possible. Place in a pan with butter, vegetable oil (allow 3 tablespoons all told for about ½ pound), a tablespoon or so of minced onion and the same amount of minced green onions. Sauté for 6 to 7 minutes over moderate heat or until mushroom pieces begin to take on some color. Season to taste with salt, pepper and freshly grated nutmeg. Finish with some minced parsley. Cool. Refrigerate in a covered jar or freeze.

No Chives?

Use the sprouting tops of onions or green onions.

Nasturtium Salad

It's summer. Your garden is awash with flowering nasturtiums. Combine both flowers and the leaves with some lettuce and toss in a Sauce Vinaigrette (page 229).

Pea Pods Are Flavor Makers

When you shell fresh peas, save the pods and cook a few along with the peas for extra flavor. Toss the rest into soups for flavoring wherever you can. Strain out after cooking.

CREAM OF PEA SOUP

2 tablespoons butter or
  margarine
2 to 3 yellow onions, peeled
  and sliced
1 cup water
1 CUP LEFTOVER GREEN PEAS
1 cup milk, about

Salt
Freshly ground white pepper
1 good teaspoon dried basil
½ cup cream
Freshly grated nutmeg
Minced parsley or mint

Heat the butter in a heavy saucepan. Add the onions and the water. Bring to a boil and cook until all the water has boiled away and the onions are tender. If necessary, add more water.

Place the onions, peas and milk (a small amount at a time) in the container of an electric blender. Purée at high speed. Pour into the saucepan, add salt and pepper to taste, and the basil. Stir in the cream and nutmeg. Taste for seasoning. If the soup turns out to be thicker than heavy cream, thin with more milk.

Serve in heated soup bowls or plates with a garnish of minced parsley or mint. Should serve around 6.

GLORIA PÉPIN'S PEPPERS

If you have a single green pepper in the refrigerator or even a half, here's a good way to use it up.

1 GREEN PEPPER, OR LESS
2 cloves garlic, crushed,
  peeled and minced

3 or 4 tablespoons olive oil
Salt
Freshly ground pepper

Pick up the pepper with a kitchen fork and hold over a high flame until the skin is black. Cut open and remove the seeds if whole; pull off the black skin. Cut in strips about ¼ inch wide.

Combine the pepper and garlic with oil, salt and pepper to taste in a bowl or jar. Refrigerate. Perfectly delicious as an hors d'oeuvre or in a salad and it keeps a long time.

HOME-FRIED POTATOES

LEFTOVER BOILED POTATOES,
  ABOUT 6
4 tablespoons (½ stick)
  butter, margarine, vegetable
  or peanut oil or beef
  drippings

Salt
Freshly ground pepper

Peel the potatoes and cut into ⅛-inch slices. Heat the butter or other fat in a large heavy skillet. Add the potatoes and brown slowly on one side. Shake the pan two or three times to move the slices around. When brown on one side, turn and brown the other. Lift to a hot serving dish. Salt and pepper to taste.

POTATO SALAD, SWEDISH STYLE

3 or 4 LEFTOVER BOILED
  POTATOES, PEELED AND
  SLICED
½ yellow onion, peeled and
  chopped

6 to 7 sprigs parsley, minced
1 tablespoon chopped chives
  or capers
½ cup diced beets
Dressing (see below)

Arrange the potato slices in a salad bowl with the onion, parsley, chives or capers and beets in rows on top. Pour the dressing over all and refrigerate for 1 to 2 hours. Toss just before serving. Good with sausage or cold meat. Serves 3.

Dressing

1 tablespoon wine vinegar
3 tablespoons olive, peanut or
   vegetable oil

Salt to taste
Freshly ground white
   pepper to taste

Place all the dressing ingredients in a bottle and shake well.

SCALLOPED POTATOES, COUNTRY STYLE

3 tablespoons butter,
   margarine or bacon fat
3 tablespoons all-purpose flour
1½ cups half and half
Salt
Freshly ground white pepper
Freshly grated nutmeg
⅓ cup grated cheese
   (Parmesan, Swiss or
   Cheddar)

2 or 3 MEDIUM LEFTOVER
   POTATOES (BOILED OR
   BAKED), CUBED
2 medium yellow onions,
   peeled, sliced thin and
   sautéed in butter
½ cup dry bread crumbs,
   mixed with 2 tablespoons
   melted butter

Preheat oven to 350°.

Butter a 2½-quart baking dish that can go to the table.

Heat the remaining butter in a heavy saucepan. Stir in the flour until smooth. Cook, stirring constantly, until the mixture froths. Add the half and half and cook, whipping constantly, until the sauce comes to a boil and thickens. Season to taste with salt, pepper and nutmeg. Stir in the cheese. Keep sauce hot over water.

Starting with potatoes, arrange vegetables in layers in a buttered baking dish, spooning some of the sauce over each layer. Sprinkle the last layer with the buttered bread crumbs.

Bake until the crumbs are brown and the scallop piping hot.

POTATO STICKS

1½ cups all-purpose flour
1½ CUPS LEFTOVER MASHED
    POTATOES

6 tablespoons (¾ stick)
    butter or margarine
2 teaspoons salt
Grated Parmesan cheese

Preheat oven to 450°.

Line a cookie sheet with kitchen parchment and set aside.

Combine flour, potatoes, butter or margarine, and salt. Roll out thin on a lightly floured board. Cut into 1-inch by 5-inch sticks, sprinkle with cheese and bake on the prepared cookie sheet for 10 to 12 minutes. Makes quite a lot.

Splendid to serve with cocktails, salad or soup.

POTATO PANCAKES

½ cup half and half
½ cup fine bread crumbs
2 CUPS LEFTOVER MASHED
    POTATOES
2 egg yolks, slightly beaten
2 teaspoons grated onion

Salt
Freshly ground pepper
Freshly grated nutmeg
Good pinch thyme
Bacon fat

Scald the half and half. Pour over the bread crumbs and let stand overnight in the refrigerator to absorb the liquid. The following day, mix the potatoes and beaten yolks together. Combine with the soaked bread crumbs and all remaining ingredients except the bacon fat.

To bake, coat two small (8-inch) skillets with bacon fat. When the fat is smoking hot, drop the potato mixture by tablespoons into the pans. Flatten immediately with a spatula so the bottom of each pan is covered completely. Cook over a low heat until the underside is well browned. Turn with a spatula (toss if you have the skill) and brown the other side. Makes 14 to 20 pancakes.

Serve piping hot with pot roast, pork chops, hamburgers or steak.

POTATO AND ONION SOUP

3 large yellow onions, peeled
and sliced
3 tablespoons butter,
margarine or fat
2 tablespoons all-purpose
flour
2 cups poultry broth
(page 59)
3 cups milk

2 CUPS LEFTOVER MASHED
POTATOES
Salt
Freshly ground white pepper
1 teaspoon fresh thyme,
minced, or ¼ teaspoon
dried
Minced parsley or chives

Combine onions and butter in a large saucepan. Sauté over moderate heat until the onions are golden. Sprinkle the flour over the mixture, then stir until smooth. Cook over a low heat until the flour and butter froth, 2 or 3 minutes. Stir in the broth, milk and potatoes. Mix thoroughly. Bring to a boil, reduce heat and simmer for about 10 minutes. Season well with salt and pepper. Stir in the thyme.

Serve piping hot in big soup plates with a garnish of parsley or chives. A hearty soup that almost makes a complete meal for 8.

A STURDY SOUP FROM SPROUTING POTATOES

SPROUTING POTATOES
1 large yellow onion, peeled
3 or 4 sprigs parsley
Salt

Peppercorns
1 or 2 bouillon cubes
Cold water to cover
Heavy cream

Cut off sprouts and wash and quarter the potatoes (skins on). Place in a heavy saucepan with the onion cut in half, the parsley, salt to taste, a few peppercorns and 1 or 2 bouillon cubes. Cover with cold water and bring to a boil. Reduce heat, cover, and simmer until potatoes are very soft. Push through a fine sieve. Taste for seasoning. Stir in a little heavy cream. The exact number of servings will depend on how many potatoes you have available.

Variations on Mashed Potatoes

Let's say you have about 2 cups of leftover mashed potatoes. Beat into them a little hot milk with a few knobs of butter. Heat thoroughly. Season to taste with salt and pepper. Now add any of the following:
Grated orange rind
Finely chopped chives
Finely chopped green onion tops
Finely chopped watercress leaves
Finely chopped parsley sprigs

Leftover Potato Crust for Meat or Vegetable Pies

This is an excellent way to use up leftover mashed potatoes. The amount of potato you will need depends, obviously, on the size of the pie plate or casserole used.

You can do several things with the potatoes:

1. Mix with butter, hot milk or cream, salt and freshly ground white pepper to taste.

2. To the above mixture you can add 1 or 2 egg yolks, slightly beaten, which makes a richer crust.

3. To the first mixture you can add 1 or 2 egg whites, stiffly beaten, which makes for a lighter crust.

4. Beat 1 egg yolk with 1 tablespoon of cream or milk and brush over the crust to give it a glossy finish.

FRENCH CHOCOLATE CAKE

5 squares (1-ounce size) unsweetened chocolate
1 teaspoon instant coffee
1/2 cup (1 stick) butter or margarine, at room temperature

1 1/2 cups sugar
2 egg yolks
1 teaspoon vanilla
2 CUPS LEFTOVER POTATOES, PURÉED AND HEATED

Cover the bottom of a 4-cup oblong dish with a piece of kitchen parchment or waxed paper. Set aside.

Combine the chocolate with the instant coffee in the top of a double boiler and melt over simmering water. Put the butter, cut up, into a bowl and beat with an electric beater until soft and creamy. Add the sugar and the egg yolks and beat until the mixture makes ribbons. Stir in the melted chocolate and vanilla. Finally, beat in the hot potatoes thoroughly.

Spoon into the prepared dish, smooth the surface and place a piece of kitchen parchment flat on top. Refrigerate until firm.

To serve, turn out on a platter and cut into very thin slices. Extremely rich, this cake will keep almost indefinitely in the refrigerator.

CREAM OF SPINACH SOUP

1 CUP LEFTOVER SPINACH,
  CHOPPED
1 tablespoon grated onion
1 to 2 cooked carrots, chopped
1 cup milk

1½ cups thick Sauce
  Béchamel (page 230)*
Salt
¼ cup heavy cream, whipped
Paprika

Purée the spinach, onion and carrots, a little at a time, with some milk and/or Béchamel, in a blender at high speed. Once the vegetables have been puréed, combine in a heavy saucepan with the remaining milk and sauce and bring to a boil. Add salt to taste. Spoon into heated soup plates, add a dollop of whipped cream and a sprinkling of paprika.

A New Taste to Leftover Spinach

Let's say you have a cup or so of cooked spinach. Squeeze dry with your hands, then chop coarsely. Season to taste with salt and freshly ground pepper. Stir in a couple of table-spoons of sour cream and a good squeeze of lemon juice. Serve with cold meat.

* Make the Sauce Béchamel in these proportions: 3 tablespoons butter or margarine; 3 tablespoons flour; 1 cup milk; salt and freshly ground white pepper to taste.

SQUASH SOUFFLÉ

Butter or margarine
Fine, dry bread crumbs
  (page 197)
2 CUPS LEFTOVER MASHED
  HUBBARD SQUASH
1 *cup thick Sauce Béchamel*
  (page 230)

Salt
Freshly ground white pepper
4 whole eggs, separated
Pinch of cream of tartar
2 extra egg whites

Preheat oven to 375°.

Butter a 1½-quart soufflé mold, including the curve at the bottom. Coat with bread crumbs, dumping out any excess. Refrigerate.

Mix the squash and Béchamel together and season with salt and pepper to taste. Add the yolks, one at a time, beating hard after each addition. The soufflé can be prepared ahead to this point and set aside, sealed with plastic wrap.

Add a good pinch of cream of tartar and a pinch of salt to the egg whites. Beat with an electric beater or in the electric mixer until they hold firm, shiny peaks when the beater is held straight up. Using a wire whip, beat about a third of the whites into the squash mixture thoroughly, then pour the mixture over the whites and fold in gently with a rubber spatula.

Pour into the prepared mold. Place on a baking sheet and bake for about 30 minutes or until the soufflé has puffed and browned lightly.

Serve immediately as an accompaniment to roast or broiled chicken, turkey, roast beef or steak.

HUBBARD SQUASH BISQUE*

2 CUPS MASHED LEFTOVER
  HUBBARD SQUASH
Salt
Freshly ground white pepper
2 or 3 tablespoons honey
3 cups chicken broth

Freshly grated nutmeg
½ cup heavy cream
Sherry or Madeira to taste
Slivered toasted almonds
  (optional)

Combine all the ingredients, except the almonds, and mix very well. As a matter of fact, you might very well do it in an electric mixer and achieve a very smooth purée. The consistency should be like that of heavy cream. Bring to a boil and serve with a garnish of slivered almonds. Makes about 6 cups.

Sweet Potato Vines

If you have one sweet potato that you don't know what to do with, place one end of it in a glass of water. It will sprout a beautiful, hardy vine that will grow to fabulous lengths all over your kitchen.

SWEET POTATO BISCUITS

¾ CUP MASHED LEFTOVER
  SWEET POTATOES
⅔ cup milk
4 tablespoons (½ stick) butter
  or margarine, melted

1¼ cups all-purpose flour
4 tablespoons baking powder
1 tablespoon brown sugar
½ teaspoon salt

Preheat oven to 450°.

* A tasty soup can also be made with an equal amount of leftover sweet potatoes instead of squash.

Combine potatoes, milk and melted butter. Mix together thoroughly. Sift the remaining ingredients together, then mix into the potato mixture to make a soft dough. Turn out onto a lightly floured pastry cloth and toss until smooth. Using a rolling pin in a floured pastry sleeve, roll out the dough to a ½-inch thickness. Cut with a biscuit cutter dipped in flour.

Place on an ungreased baking sheet and bake 12 to 20 minutes or until golden. Makes about 15 biscuits.

Too Many Tomatoes?

Anyone who has even the smallest garden patch is bound to have three or four tomato plants in it. The experienced gardener knows that come late summer, these plants will yield more fruit than your family can possibly consume in salads. You'll end up carting the excess off to friends and neighbors or, heaven forbid, letting it rot on the vines. The recipes that follow are intended to help you use your harvest without getting sick of tomatoes or wasting a single fat red precious globe.

TOMATO JUICE

If you have a quantity of tomatoes that are going soft, they are at an ideal stage to make tomato juice. Three pounds will yield about 1 quart of juice.

Wash, pull off the stems and cut out any spots. Chop coarsely. Place in a large kettle and bring to a boil. Reduce heat, cover and simmer for 5 to 10 minutes or until the juices flow freely. Push through a fine sieve, pressing the pulp to squeeze out all the juices. Discard pulp. Season with salt, allowing about 1 teaspoon per quart of juice. Pour into pint refrigerator containers, leaving space at the top. Cover securely and freeze. Note: Freezer must retain zero temperature.

RATATOUILLE

⅓ cup olive oil
2 cloves garlic, crushed,
    peeled and minced
1 large yellow onion, peeled
    and sliced
½ cup water
3 tablespoons all-purpose flour
2 zucchini, washed and thinly
    sliced

1 small eggplant, skin on,
    thinly sliced
2 green or red sweet peppers,
    seeded, ribs removed, thinly
    sliced
5 RIPE TOMATOES, PEELED,
    SEEDED AND CHOPPED
Salt
Freshly ground black pepper
1 tablespoon capers, drained

Heat the oil in a large skillet. Add the garlic, onion and water. Cook until all the water has boiled away and the onion is transparent.

Flour the zucchini and eggplant lightly, shaking off any excess. Add to the skillet along with the peppers. Cover and cook over low heat for 1 hour. Add the tomatoes and simmer, uncovered, until the mixture is very thick. Season to taste with salt and pepper. Add the capers 15 minutes before the ratatouille has finished cooking. Serve hot or cold to 4 or 5.

TOMATOES ANDALUSIAN

4 MEDIUM-SIZE RIPE TOMATOES
Salt
Freshly ground pepper
2 tablespoons peanut,
    vegetable or olive oil
1 small yellow onion, peeled
    and minced

½ sweet green pepper, seeds
    and ribs removed, minced
1 cup cooked rice
Mayonnaise
Lettuce

Cut a slice off the ends of the tomatoes. Scoop out and discard the centers, leaving the shells intact. Sprinkle the cavities with salt and pepper and allow to stand for half an hour. Invert on paper towels to drain.

Heat the oil in a skillet. Add the onion and pepper and sauté until limp but not brown. Combine with rice and enough mayonnaise to hold the mixture together. Season to taste with salt and pepper. Chill. Fill the tomato shells and serve on lettuce leaves.

TOMATOES STUFFED WITH POTATOES AND SWISS CHEESE

4 MEDIUM-SIZE RIPE TOMATOES	¾ cup diced boiled potatoes
Salt	¾ cup diced Swiss cheese
Freshly ground pepper	1 tablespoon minced onion
Lots of chopped chives	Mayonnaise

Cut the tomatoes in half and scoop out and discard centers. Turn upside down to drain. Sprinkle cavities with salt, pepper and chopped chives. Combine the remaining ingredients with enough mayonnaise to hold the mixture together. Fill the tomatoes and garnish with chives.

TURNIP AND POTATO SOUP

1 large yellow onion, peeled and chopped	2 CUPS LEFTOVER MASHED YELLOW TURNIPS (RUTABAGAS)
2 to 3 tablespoons butter or margarine	2 cups mashed potatoes
1 cup water	Milk or cream
1 to 2 cups poultry broth (page 59)	Salt
	Freshly ground pepper
	Croutons (page 197) or minced parsley

Place the onion, butter or margarine and water in a small pan. Bring to a boil. Boil until all the water has evaporated and the onion is soft and transparent. Purée in an electric blender with a cup or so of the broth. Mix the turnips and potatoes together and blend thoroughly into the purée. Add enough milk or cream to bring the mixture to a thick soup consistency. Season to taste with salt and pepper. Bring the soup to a boil.

Serve piping hot in heated soup plates with a garnish of croutons or minced parsley. Makes better than 8 cups depending on how much milk is added.

WATERCRESS STEM SOUP

Watercress stems from 1 bunch
2 tablespoons butter or margarine
½ yellow onion, peeled and coarsely chopped

1 tablespoon all-purpose flour
3 cups poultry broth (page 59)
1 cup heavy cream or milk
Salt
Freshly ground pepper

Cut the watercress leaves off the stems and refrigerate in a plastic bag to use in salad. Chop the stems coarsely.

Heat the butter in a heavy kettle. Add the onion and watercress stems. Cook about 2 minutes, stirring. Sprinkle in the flour. Cook until the mixture froths, about 3 more minutes. Add the chicken broth and simmer 10 minutes. Blend in an electric blender, a small amount at a time. Return to the kettle and add heavy cream or milk. Season to taste with salt and freshly ground pepper. Should serve about 6.

Mayonnaise Cresson

This is a delicious way to use the stems of a bunch of watercress, when the leaves are used in salad. Mince the stems very fine and mix them into mayonnaise. Then combine with lemon juice.

Serve with hot Fish Soufflé (page 104) or broiled fillets of sole.

Save Liquids from Canned and Home-cooked Vegetables

Add to soups, savory sauces, stews, gravies, casserole dishes or creamed sauces to be served with vegetables.

How to Use Up Odds and Ends of Cooked Vegetables

When you serve vegetables hot such as peas, beans, carrots, etc., don't dress them beforehand with butter or margarine because any that are left over can be added to your salad the following day.

RICE, BEANS
AND PASTA

Storing Breakfast Cereals, Other Grains and Pasta

The United States Department of Agriculture recommends the following:

> Breakfast cereals, 2 to 3 months
> Bulgar, 6 months
> Corn meal and hominy grits, 4 to 6 months
> Pasta (except noodles), 1 year
> Egg noodles, 6 months
> Rice (white, parboiled, precooked), 1 year
> Brown rice, 6 months

To Freeze Leftover Rice

If you have cooked too much rice, cool, spoon into a suitable freezer container and freeze. To thaw, cover with boiling water or broth and bring to a boil. Do not cook further. Drain off water, but if broth is used drain into a bowl to use again. Or pour into a freezer container and freeze.

Uses for Leftover Rice

In Soups

Add leftover rice to soups or broth.

In Meat Loaf

Replace bread crumbs in meat loaf with same amount of cooked rice.

In Chowder
Add leftover rice to fish chowder just before serving.

With Eggs
Add ½ cup or so of leftover rice to scrambled eggs along with leftover vegetables such as peas or green beans. A good hearty lunch for the kids.

For Breakfast
Warm leftover rice in enough butter to coat it, stirring constantly. Place the buttered rice in a mound on a hot plate and top with a poached egg. Nice change for breakfast or even lunch.

Stuffing for Celery
Mix a little mayonnaise with leftover rice, add a squeeze of lemon juice and lots of chopped chives. Stuff ribs of celery.

In Salad
Mix rice with chopped hard-cooked eggs, chopped green or ripe olives and a little minced onion. Toss with Sauce Vinaigrette (page 229).

Make a New Rice Dessert
Combine leftover cold plain white rice with chocolate, vanilla or butterscotch pudding. If you have a few pecans or walnuts on hand, chop them up and add them, too.

RICE STUFFING FOR MEAT, FISH OR FOWL

2 tablespoons butter or fat	*2 to 3 sprigs parsley, minced*
1 tablespoon chopped onion	*Salt*
½ cup diced celery	*Freshly ground pepper*
1 CUP LEFTOVER RICE	*Worcestershire sauce*

Melt the butter in a skillet. Add the onion and celery and sauté until tender but not browned. Add to rice and mix in parsley. Season with salt, pepper and Worcestershire sauce to taste.

RICE PATTIES

2 CUPS LEFTOVER RICE
¼ cup shredded Cheddar
  cheese (about 1 ounce)
2 tablespoons fine dry bread
  crumbs
5 to 6 sprigs parsley

1 whole egg plus 1 egg yolk,
  beaten together
Salt
Freshly ground pepper
Bacon drippings, butter or
  margarine

Mix all ingredients except fat together until thoroughly blended. Shape into about 6 patties.

Heat the fat in a skillet and fry the patties until golden on both sides. Very good with fried chicken.

RICE CORN BREAD

4 tablespoons (½ stick) butter
  or margarine, melted
1 cup corn meal
2½ teaspoons baking powder

1 teaspoon salt
1 CUP COOKED LEFTOVER RICE
1 egg, well beaten
1 cup cold milk

Preheat oven to 400°.

Pour half the melted butter in a 9-inch by 9-inch by 2½-inch baking pan. Set aside.

Combine the corn meal, baking powder and salt in a sifter. Sift over the cooked rice. Mix well with a fork, separating the rice kernels. Combine the beaten egg and milk. Stir well into the rice mixture alternately with the remaining butter.

Pour into the baking pan and again mix well. Bake for 30 to 40 minutes or until nicely browned. Serve, cut into wedges, with loads of sweet butter. Serves 6.

BAKED RICE AND CHEESE

2 tablespoons melted butter
  or margarine
3 eggs, separated
1 CUP COLD LEFTOVER RICE

¾ cup shredded Cheddar
  cheese
½ cup milk
Pinch salt

Preheat oven to 375°.

Butter a 1½-quart baking dish and set aside.

Beat the egg yolks well and stir into the rice. Stir in all remaining ingredients except the egg whites. Beat the whites until they hold firm, shiny peaks when the beater is held straight up. Fold into the rice mixture and pour into the prepared dish.

Bake for about 35 minutes or until set. Serves 4 or thereabouts.

QUICK RICE PUDDING*

¾ CUP LEFTOVER RICE
¾ cup milk
¾ cup seedless raisins
1 egg, separated

3 tablespoons sugar
1 teaspoon vanilla
⅛ teaspoon salt

Combine rice, milk and raisins in a saucepan. Mix together the egg yolk, 2 tablespoons of the sugar, the vanilla and salt.

---

* To make a chocolate-flavored pudding, add ½ square (1-ounce size) unsweetened chocolate, melted in the top of a double boiler, to the milk before combining with rice, and skip the raisins.

Stir into rice mixture. Cook over medium heat, stirring constantly, until mixture comes to a boil. Reduce heat to low and cook, again stirring constantly, until thick and creamy—about 5 minutes. Take off the heat and cool (quickly done in the freezer).

Beat the egg white until it begins to hold a shape. Then beat in the remaining tablespoon of sugar. Fold into the cooled rice.

Serve with whipped cream or yoghurt to 3 or possibly 4.

MAPLE RICE PUDDING

½ cup heavy cream
⅓ cup real maple syrup

1½ CUPS LEFTOVER RICE, AT
ROOM TEMPERATURE
Pinch salt

Whip the cream until it just holds a shape, then mix in the syrup. Fold in the rice and a good pinch of salt. Pour into a 2-cup serving bowl and refrigerate. Stir once during the first half hour. Serve with a pitcher of cream.

WHITE BEAN SALAD

Any of the white bean family can be used in this salad—marrow, great Northern, navy or pea. The marrow is the largest and the pea the smallest.

1 clove garlic, unpeeled and
  split
1½ CUPS LEFTOVER WHITE
  BEANS
½ medium yellow onion,
  peeled and minced or 4 or
  5 green onion bulbs, minced
Handful parsley sprigs,
  minced

3 tablespoons oil
1 tablespoon wine vinegar
Salt to taste
Freshly ground white pepper
  to taste
Garnish:
  Minced parsley or red onion
  rings or both

Rub a salad bowl with the garlic clove and then discard the used clove. Add the beans and all remaining ingredients except garnish. Toss well. Allow the salad to stand for a couple of hours. Add the garnish just before serving.

MACARONI SALAD, SAUCE VINAIGRETTE

2 CUPS LEFTOVER MACARONI
1 small yellow onion, peeled
  and minced
8 to 10 sprigs parsley, minced
1 cucumber, peeled and diced

Sauce Vinaigrette (page 229)
Romaine lettuce
2 large ripe tomatoes, cut in
  wedges

Combine the macaroni, onion, parsley and cucumber in a salad bowl. Make the Sauce Vinaigrette. Pour over the mixture and toss to coat well. Marinate in the refrigerator for at least 30 minutes.

To serve, tuck the lettuce leaves under the salad and garnish with tomato wedges. Serves 3 to 4.

BREAD, CAKE AND PASTRY

Ways to Use Stale Bread

Stale Bread

Here are several ways to make the most of bread that's going stale.

Croutons

Cut the bread in small cubes. Bake in a preheated 275° oven until crisp and lightly browned. Serve with soup.

Soft bread crumbs

Break up the bread, place in a blender and grate into soft crumbs. Soft crumbs are called for in some stuffings, but not all. They are also used to coat some foods that are to be deep-fat fried.

Dry bread crumbs

Place the bread on a baking sheet in a preheated 200° oven until brittle but not brown. Grate in an electric blender. Dry crumbs are used in stuffings, especially when there are other solid ingredients such as ground or chopped meats, mushrooms, etc. They are also used to finish casseroles and to crumb meat and fish.

Baked toast

If you are being elegant cut off the crusts and then cut the bread into triangles. Butter well, place on a baking sheet in a preheated 300° oven and bake until golden brown, 20 to 30 minutes. Serve with salads or soups.

Crusts

Always save the crusts because you can dry, grate and combine them with dry bread crumbs.

Croustades

You can make golden croustades from stale bread. Slice loaves of firm stale white bread about 2½ inches thick. Cut off the crusts and scoop out the centers, leaving a shell ½ inch thick. Save centers and crusts (see above). Brush the shells with melted butter or margarine. Place on a baking sheet and bake in a preheated 350° oven for 15 to 20 minutes or until golden brown. A delicious substitute for patty shells.

Freshening Stale Bread

Rolls, French bread or muffins can be revived by sprinkling them with water, placing in a brown paper bag and heating in a hot oven for a few minutes. Or place on a piece of foil, cover with a couple of lettuce leaves (a good way to make use of leaves that are wilted) bring the foil up and press together. Heat in a hot oven.

BREAD STUFFING FOR POULTRY

You should allow about 1 cup of dressing per pound of bird. So, this recipe makes sufficient stuffing for a 4-pound chicken.

½ cup (1 stick) butter or
   margarine (about)
½ small yellow onion, peeled
   and minced, or ½ cup
   peeled and minced green
   onion bulbs

2 CUPS FRESH BREAD CRUMBS*
1 teaspoon dried tarragon
Handful parsley sprigs,
   minced
Salt to taste
Freshly ground pepper

Place the butter in a heavy skillet. When hot, add the onion and ½ cup water. Bring to a boil and cook until all the water has boiled away and the onion is soft. Stir in the bread crumbs. Mix with the herbs, and salt and pepper to taste.

Variations

With *sausage meat*. Allow about ¾ pound of sausage to 4 cups of bread crumbs. Reduce the butter content by 2 tablespoons.

With *nuts*. Allow about ½ cup toasted almonds or pine nuts to 4 cups of bread crumbs.

With *parsley and lemon*. Allow the grated rind and juice of 1 lemon, the minced sprigs from a good bunch of parsley, ½ teaspoon dried marjoram and 2 whole eggs to 4 cups bread crumbs.

BREAD PUDDING

3 tablespoons butter or
   margarine
2 CUPS CUBED FIRM WHITE
   BREAD
⅓ cup seedless raisins
   (optional)

1 quart milk, scalded
2 eggs, or 4 yolks
⅓ cup sugar
½ teaspoon salt
1 teaspoon vanilla

* 1 piece of firm white bread with crusts makes ¼ cup bread crumbs.

Preheat oven to 350°.

Butter a 1-quart baking dish well and set aside. Place the cubes of bread and raisins in a large bowl and add the hot milk. Allow to soak for 30 minutes.

Combine the eggs, sugar and salt and beat slightly. Mix into the bread mixture along with any remaining butter and vanilla.

Pour into the prepared baking dish, place in a baking pan and add enough hot water from the tap to reach to two- thirds the depth of the mold. Bake for 1 hour and 15 minutes or until a knife inserted one inch from the center comes out clean. Serve warm.

FRENCH TOAST
(*Pain Perdu*)

DAY-OLD BREAD (PREFERABLY FRENCH)
Milk
Sugar
Vanilla
Grand Marnier (optional)
Beaten eggs
Flour
Butter or margarine

Soak slices of day-old bread in a little lukewarm milk sweetened with a few tablespoons of sugar and flavored with a few drops of vanilla, and if you like, Grand Marnier.

Beat the eggs in a soup plate. Dip the soaked bread into the beaten eggs, then in the flour. Shake off any excess flour.

Fry in butter until golden on both sides. Sprinkle liberally with sugar or serve topped with a lump of butter.

PARMESAN AND BEER CROUTONS
TO SERVE WITH DRINKS OR SOUPS

Cold beer
Freshly grated Parmesan
   cheese

Good pinch cayenne pepper
CROUTONS (page 197)
Melted butter

Preheat oven to 450°.

Pour a small amount of beer into a small bowl. Mix the cheese and cayenne together. Dip the croutons into the beer, then roll them in the cheese mixture. Place on a baking sheet lined with kitchen parchment or buttered waxed paper. Sprinkle with the melted butter and bake, turning them as they brown, for 10 minutes.

GARLIC CHEESE STICKS

A dandy way to use up a few slices of dry white bread.

4 SLICES DRY WHITE BREAD
1 clove garlic, crushed and
   peeled

½ cup sweet butter, cut into
   pieces
Grated Parmesan cheese or
   sesame or poppy seeds

Preheat oven to 350°.

Trim off the crusts from bread and cut each slice into 4 "fingers." Heat garlic with butter in a saucepan for 1 minute. Discard the garlic and brush the fingers on all sides with the garlic butter. Roll in Parmesan cheese or seeds, place on a baking sheet and bake for 15 minutes, or until nicely browned.

Ways to Use Stale Cake

SIMONE BECK'S POMMES DE TERRE

This is a French pastry chef's terminology for petite fours made with cake crumbs. You can make the crumbs from leftover sponge or pound cake.

2 CUPS DRY CAKE CRUMBS

1 cup ground almonds

1 egg

4 tablespoons sugar

¼ cup dark rum

Unsweetened cocoa

Take cake crumbs and mix with ground almonds. Beat egg with sugar and dark rum. Combine with the crumbs. Allow the mixture to dry. Then shape like tiny potatoes about 2 inches long and roll in unsweetened cocoa.

TRIFLE

2 LARGE PIECES STALE POUND
   CAKE OR OTHER PLAIN RICH
   CAKE

¼ cup sherry

¼ cup brandy

½ cup strawberry or raspberry
   jam

2 cups Crème Anglaise
   (page 144)

1 cup heavy cream

¼ cup slivered, toasted
   almonds

Cut the cake into 2-inch squares and sprinkle with the combined sherry and brandy. Spread each piece with jam, place in a large serving bowl and allow to stand for a couple of hours.

Meanwhile, make the Crème Anglaise. Pour the hot custard over the soaked cake and chill. Just before serving, whip the cream and spoon over the top, then scatter with almonds. Serves 8.

Ways to Use Leftover Pastry Dough

CHEESE STICKS

Let's say you have as much leftover pastry as you can gather up in a ball in one hand.

Roll dough out thin on a lightly floured board. Cover with a finely grated cheese such as Cheddar or Swiss. Fold and roll at least twice more, sprinkling with cheese each time. Cut into 3-inch by 2-inch "fingers." Place on a baking sheet. Beat 1 egg yolk lightly, adding enough salt to give it a salty taste, and use it to brush the fingers. Bake in a preheated 425° oven for 7 to 10 minutes, or until golden brown.

No cheese? Roll plain dough into fingers and bake as directed. Serve with soup.

SUGAR COOKIES FROM LEFTOVER PASTRY DOUGH

ABOUT A HANDFUL OF   *Sugar*
LEFTOVER PASTRY DOUGH

Preheat oven to 375°.

Roll the dough out about ¼inch thick and cut into circles with a 1½-inch cookie cutter. Now heap some sugar on your pastry board. Place one of the pastry rounds on top, pile more sugar on top, then roll into an oval about 2½ inches long. Repeat with each cookie until all the dough is used, adding more sugar as it is needed. Place the cookies on an ungreased cookie sheet and bake for 15 to 20 minutes or until lightly browned. Cool on a cake rack. Easy and delicious.

Crêpes

Like omelets, crêpes are a perfect way to serve leftovers and create an elegant meal. A basic recipe for crêpe batter is included here, along with some suggestions for fillings. But use your imagination also. The finished crêpes make an hors d'oeuvre or main course.

BASIC SAVORY CRÊPE BATTER

2 cups milk
4 eggs
2 cups all-purpose flour

½ teaspoon salt
4 tablespoons melted butter

Place all the ingredients in an electric blender or electric food processor and blend at high speed until you have a smooth batter—about 30 seconds. Scrape down the sides, and if necessary, blend another 15 seconds. It should have the consistency of heavy cream.

Refrigerate for at least a couple of hours, or better, over-night. Makes about a dozen 6-inch crêpes or 16 to 18 4- to 5-inch crêpes.

Dessert Crêpes

To make sweet crêpes, follow the same recipe, adding 1 table-spoon sugar and 3 tablespoons of orange liqueur, dark rum or Cognac.

HOW TO BAKE CRÊPES

You need a seasoned cast-iron crêpe pan. They are imported from France and measure from 5 to 10 inches.

Brush the pan with vegetable oil.

Place over moderately high heat until the pan is hot enough. Test with a few drops of cold water. If they bounce and sputter, the pan is right.

Take the pan off the heat. Holding the handle in your right hand, use your left hand to add a tablespoon of batter. Quickly tilt the pan in all directions so the bottom is completely covered with a thin film.

Note well: your first crêpe is a trial run, as it were, to test the consistency of your batter, the exact amount needed for the pan you are working with, and the heat.

Return the pan to the heat for about 1 minute, maybe a few seconds longer. Gently lift the edge with a spatula to determine if the underside of the crêpe is nicely and lightly brown. If so, turn. The easiest way is to pick up the edge of the crêpe with your fingers and flip it over. Brown the second side for only about 30 seconds. It will not, you will discover, brown all over but, rather, "freckle."

Place the finished crêpes on a plate with pieces of waxed paper between. If the crêpes are not going to be used immediately, keep warm in a preheated keep-warm (140°) oven until needed.

Once you become accustomed to cooking crêpes, you will soon be able to keep two or three pans going at the same time.

Crêpes will keep refrigerated for several days or they can be frozen.

HOW TO FILL CRÊPES

Place a tablespoon or so of the hot filling in each crêpe and roll up like a jelly roll. Place in a serving dish, seam side down.

The savory crêpes can be finished, if you like, with a sprinkling of cheese, melted butter or a coating of sauce, then placed in a hot oven briefly.

FILLINGS FOR SAVORY CRÊPES

Creamed Vegetables
Use such vegetables as leftover cooked peas, carrots or mushrooms. Combine with Sauce Béchamel (page 230) and season to taste with salt and freshly ground pepper. Obviously, the amount of sauce depends on the quantity of vegetable. To give you a clue, add 1 cup of the vegetables to ½ cup of the sauce.

Chicken
See Chopped Chicken and Livers with Mushrooms (page 67).

Turkey
See Turkey Mornay (page 83). Prepare the recipe without the bread crumbs and cheese, and obviously, do not bake. See Turkey Amandine (page 82).

Fish

Combine any flaked leftover fish with enough Sauce Velouté
(page 231), made with fish broth, to bind the fish. Season to
taste with salt and freshly ground white pepper. See Salt Cod
in Scallop Shells (page 110). Eliminate the bread crumbs, and
do not bake.

Sweet Crêpes

Coat one slice of each crêpe with currant jelly, strawberry jam
or apricot jam. Roll up like a jelly roll. Place, seam side down,
in a skillet or fireproof dish. Heat a bit of a liqueur (orange,
dark rum or Cognac) and ignite. Pour over the crêpes. Shake the
pan or dish until the flames die out. Serve at once.

FRUITS

Buying and Storing
Fresh Fruits

Fresh fruits should be used as soon after purchase as possible when they are at their most flavorful best. Because fruits are fragile they need special handling to keep them from being crushed or bruised. The softened tissues of bruised or crushed fruit allow spoilage organisms to penetrate the fruit and thus quickly break down the quality. Always sort fruits before storing because bruised or decaying fruit will contaminate sound, firm fruit.

Here is a general guide on buying and storing from the U. S. Department of Agriculture.

Remember, all fruits taste best at room temperature.

Apples
Refrigerate mellow apples uncovered. Unripe or hard apples are best held at cool room temperature (60° to 70°) until ready to eat. When you peel apples save the skin and freeze it for use later.

Use ripe apples within a month.

Apricots, Nectarines and Peaches
Usually ripe at time of purchase. If not, store at room temperature until they feel soft when pressed, then refrigerate.

Use within 3 to 5 days.

Avocados, Bananas and Pears
Ripen at room temperature, then refrigerate. The skin on

bananas will darken, but the flesh will remain flavorful and firm.

Use within 3 to 5 days.

Berries and Cherries
Refrigerate covered to prevent loss of moisture. Do not wash or stem until ready to use.

Use within 2 to 3 days.

Cranberries
Refrigerate covered.

Use within 1 week.

Grapes
Grapes are ready to use when you buy them. Keep refrigerated.

Use within 3 to 5 days.

Citrus Fruits
Oranges, grapefruit and lemons are best stored at cool room temperature (60° to 70°) or refrigerated uncovered.

Use within 2 weeks.

Melons
Keep at room temperature until ripe, then refrigerate. When storing cut melon, seal the cut side with plastic wrap and refrigerate.

Pineapples
This fruit will not ripen further after it has been picked. Avoid pineapples with shriveled crowns, dull brown color or bruised spots. Look for heavy pineapples; they are usually the better quality. Further, ripe pineapples have a fragrant, fruity perfume. Once cut, pineapple can be stored in a tightly covered container 2 to 3 days.

Use pineapple as soon as possible.

Plums
Usually ripe when purchased. Keep refrigerated.

Use within 3 to 5 days.

How to Store Canned Fruits and Fruit Juices
Once canned fruits and canned fruit juices have been opened, cover securely and refrigerate. They can be safely stored in their original containers but for better flavor, storage in glass or plastic is recommended.

How to Store Dried Fruits
Keep in tightly closed containers. In a cool place they'll keep about 6 months. In warm, humid weather refrigeration is recommended.

How to Store Reconstituted Fruit Juices
Once reconstituted, refrigerate in glass or plastic containers securely covered.

How to Store Jellies, Jams and Preserves
Once opened, use foil or plastic wrap underneath the cap of the jar and refrigerate. Watch them, however, because they can and will, in due course, mildew.

Easy, Delicious Way to Salvage Aging Apples
Wash the apples and pull out and discard the stems. Place in a baking dish, cover tightly, and bake in a preheated 375° oven for 50 minutes. Once cooked, scrape the apple purée off the skins and cores. Stir in enough sugar to taste. Serve as you would any applesauce. Easy?

APPLE AND POTATO SALAD

2 or 3 medium leftover
  potatoes, peeled and diced
  small
1 EATING APPLE, CORED AND
  DICED
½ small yellow onion, peeled
  and minced

About ½ cup mayonnaise
  page (139)*
Salt
Freshly ground white pepper
Lettuce

Combine all the ingredients except the lettuce and mix with
enough mayonnaise to hold the mixture together. Season well
with salt and pepper.

Arrange in a salad bowl with a garland of lettuce leaves.
Serves 3 or 4.

Very good with cold pork or chicken.

APPLE SOUP

Let's say you have 3 or 4 apples that are beginning to show
their age and you've frozen the skins of any apples you've
peeled; follow me and turn these assets into an interesting
soup.

* If you are using commercial mayonnaise add the juice of ½ lemon,
strained, and if on hand, a tablespoon or so of sour cream.

2 or 3 apples, cored and
  chopped coarsely
LEFTOVER APPLE PEELINGS
  (FROZEN)
4 cups poultry (page 59) or
  meat (page 10) broth

3 or 4 whole cloves
Small piece fresh ginger root
  (optional)*
Salt
Freshly ground white pepper
Croutons (page 197)

Combine the apples, apple peelings, broth, cloves and ginger in a large heavy saucepan. Bring slowly to a boil, then simmer until the apples are very soft. Push through a fine sieve or food mill. Discard skins, seeds, etc. Rinse out the saucepan and return the broth. Season well with salt and pepper and bring to a boil. Serve immediately in heated soup cups with a garnish of croutons. Serves 5 or 6.

CIDER SHERBET

THE PEEL FROM 4 OR 5
  LEFTOVER APPLES, CHOPPED
  COARSELY
2 cups cider

1 cup applesauce
Juice of 2 lemons, strained
2 cups syrup**

Purée the apple peel with a cup or so of the cider in an electric blender. Combine with the applesauce, remaining cider, lemon juice and the syrup. Taste to see if there is sufficient sugar.

Pour into two ice-cube trays and place in the freezer. When the ice has frozen around the edges pour into a large bowl. Beat with an electric or rotary beater. Return to the trays and continue to freeze until hard. Serves 6 to 8 people.

* ¼ teaspoon powdered ginger can be substituted for fresh.
** *To make the syrup:* Combine 2 cups of sugar with 1 cup of water in a saucepan. Bring to a boil, reduce heat somewhat, then boil until the syrup reaches 220° on a candy thermometer. Makes about 2 cups.

Be Thrifty with the Rind
from Oranges, Lemons and Grapefruit

When you use the juice of lemons, oranges or grapefruit, first salvage the rind for future use (see Candied Citrus Rind, page 217, for technique). It freezes perfectly stored in a small, tightly covered jar, such as a clean herb or spice jar. The grated rind can also be frozen (many recipes call for it) and in this case, wrap each batch in a bit of foil before storing it in a tightly covered jar.

How to Get the Most Out of a Lemon
or an Orange

You want to use the rind only? Okay, peel it, then drop the fruit in boiling water for a couple of minutes. This yields more juice—as much as a tablespoon more! Pour into a midget container or an individual ice-cube container and freeze. Be sure to mark it or you may get it mixed up with your frozen egg whites (page 127) which, I speak from experience, is a disaster.

You want to use the juice? Peel off the rind or grate it. If you peeled it, place rind in small glass jar, cover and freeze. If you grated it, place the grated rind in a piece of foil (not waxed paper), then in a covered glass jar, and freeze against the day when a recipe calls for grated rind. Before squeezing the fruit, give it the heat treatment (see above).

If only a squirt of fruit juice is needed? Make a little hole with a toothpick in the fruit and squeeze out exactly what you need.

Dry your orange rinds. Using a swivel-bladed vegetable peeler, peel off the rind (skip the white because it's bitter) and spread out to dry. Left out in the open, rind will dry in a few days to a week, depending on the humidity. Eight large oranges will yield about 4 ounces of dried rind. Use in recipes calling for dried orange rinds.

CANDIED CITRUS RIND

The rind from oranges, lemons or grapefruits makes a perfectly delicious candy that can also be used as a garnish on cakes, fruit compotes, etc. Some French chefs I know literally gobble them up when they come to see me. So, I hide them.

Using a swivel-bladed vegetable peeler, cut the rind off the fruit in wide strips, taking care not to pick up any of the white inner skin. Using a sharp knife, cut rind in long very thin strips or julienne. Easily done by piling a few strips on top of each other, then cutting down the entire length.

1½ cups sugar	RIND FROM 4 LARGE ORANGES,
1 cup water	6 TO 8 LEMONS OR 3
	GRAPEFRUIT

Combine 1 cup of the sugar and water in a heavy saucepan. Bring to a boil. Add the rind and cook over moderate heat for 35 to 40 minutes or until *most* of the syrup has evaporated. Watch carefully so the rind doesn't stick to the pan and scorch. A Flame Tamer (page 61) under the saucepan is a big help.

Meanwhile, sprinkle the other ½ cup of sugar on a baking sheet or tray. Once the rind is cooked, lift with a kitchen fork to the tray of sugar. Separate the pieces with the fork and mix with the sugar until the rind is well coated. Then place on a wire rack to dry. Store in airtight containers.

LEMON SAUCE*

½ *cup sugar*
1 *tablespoon cornstarch*
Pinch salt
1 *cup water*
2 *tablespoons leftover lemon*
  juice, strained

1 TEASPOON GRATED LEFTOVER
  LEMON RIND
2 *tablespoons butter or*
  margarine

Combine the sugar, cornstarch, salt and water in a medium saucepan. Stir over a moderate heat until the mixture has thickened and is clear. Take off the heat and stir in the remaining ingredients. Serve over plain cake, puddings, etc. Makes about 1¼ cups.

SIMONE BECK'S VIN D'ORANGE**

DRIED LEFTOVER RIND FROM 8
  LARGE ORANGES (PAGE 216)
2 *whole cloves*
Small piece cinnamon stick

1 *bottle dry white wine*
  (4/5 *quart*)
Sugar to taste
2 *to 3 tablespoons Cognac*

Place the rind in a 1½-quart bottle. Add the cloves and the cinnamon stick. Add the wine and cork tightly. Set in a cool place, out of the light, to steep for 8 to 10 days. Strain. Pour 1 cup into a saucepan, add sugar to taste and stir over low heat until the sugar has dissolved. Do not boil. Pour back into the wine in the bottle. Add the Cognac. Shake gently to mix.

Serve cold with a sliver of fresh orange rind in each glass.

---

* To make Lemon Sauce Mousseline, pour cold Lemon Sauce over 1 cup whipped heavy cream and fold in with a rubber spatula. Serve on cake and cold puddings, and dessert soufflés, etc.
** From SIMCA'S CUISINE, by Simone Beck and Patricia Simon. Copyright © 1972 by Simone Beck and Patricia Simon. Reprinted by permission of Alfred A. Knopf, Inc.

RAISIN SAUCE

If you have some raisins or currants dried to a nubbin you can turn them into a nice sauce.

¾ cup sugar   *Dash of lemon juice*
1 cup water   DRIED RAISINS OR CURRANTS

Combine sugar, water and lemon juice in a small saucepan. Bring to a boil and boil for 5 minutes. Add raisins or currants. Allow to stand until they plump up. Serve hot or cold over ice cream. Keeps almost indefinitely refrigerated.

FRESH STRAWBERRY GLAZE

1 *egg yolk, beaten very well*   6 TABLESPOONS PURÉED FRESH
2 *tablespoons butter or*   STRAWBERRIES
   margarine, melted   ½ *cup sifted confectioners'*
                                         sugar

Mix all ingredients together thoroughly. Spread a thin layer of the glaze over the top of a cake with a knife. Then spoon dribbles of the glaze over and down the sides. Allow to stand at room temperature until dry. Especially attractive over Angel Cake (page 137).

How to Turn Soft Strawberries into a Sauce

Sometimes strawberries are too soft to serve whole. In which case, wash, hull, chop coarsely and purée in the blender. Sweeten with superfine sugar. Use as a sauce over ice cream or pound cake or with a hot lemon soufflé.

Jelly Sauce

If you have the tail end of a jar of jelly—say, ½ cup or less—
put it in a small saucepan. Break it up with a fork, then mix
in a generous tablespoon of hot water. Stir over low heat until
the jelly has melted. A nice easy little sauce for cake or
puddings.

BEVERAGES

ANITA'S COFFEE BREAD PUDDING

Straight out of a thrifty Belgian kitchen comes this idea for using up the coffee left over from breakfast to make a pudding for dinner.

1 loaf stale French or Italian
    bread (about 10 ounces)
2½ CUPS LEFTOVER COFFEE*
1 cup raisins
6 tablespoons (¾ stick) butter
    or margarine, softened
¾ cup brown sugar

1 teaspoon vanilla extract
2 eggs, slightly beaten
¼ teaspoon cinnamon
Glaze:
   1 cup confectioners' sugar
   2 tablespoons water

Preheat oven to 375°.

Line an 8-inch round cake pan with kitchen parchment. Set aside.

Break up the bread and place in a bowl. Add the coffee and allow to soak for about 20 minutes. At the same time, cover the raisins with water to plump them up. Once plumped, drain. Combine the bread and drained raisins, and all remaining ingredients. Mix together with your hands.

Pour into the prepared pan and bake for 1 hour or until a knife inserted in the center comes out dry, that is, without any

---

* If you haven't sufficient coffee, add enough milk to make up the difference.

batter clinging to it. Turn out on a cake rack. Then reverse onto a serving plate and glaze.

Glaze: Mix sifted confectioners' sugar with water until smooth. Spread over the cake with metal spatula.

To Freeze Leftover Coffee and Tea

Pour leftover coffee or tea into midget freezer containers or individual plastic ice-cube containers and freeze. Add to iced coffee or tea as you would ice cubes.

Leftover Coffee Grounds?

A layer of coffee grounds on top of your house plant soil will help to regulate its acidity. Further, with vegetable and fruit parings, they make a fertile mulch for your indoor and outdoor garden.

Using Up "Turned" Wine

If you discover a wine has turned and is no longer drinkable, it can be used in a marinade (page 4) to tenderize meats, and its acidity makes it an excellent replacement for vinegar in the marinade. Turned wines are excellent for this purpose and it doesn't seem to matter how much time has elapsed since the wine turned.

A Few Drops of Wine

If there are a couple of tablespoons of wine left in the bottle following a dinner, add them to your vinegar bottle—red with red, white with white.

Wines and Liquors as Part of the Liquid

These add flavor to many dishes, particularly meats or fowl. But remember that because a little wine is good in a dish, a lot is not necessarily better.

HARD CIDER SAUCE

If you have a bit of leftover pork or ham you want to dress up, try this sauce. It's awfully good.

3 tablespoons butter or margarine	3 tablespoons all-purpose flour
3 tablespoons chopped onion	1 teaspoon dry mustard
3 tablespoons chopped celery	1 CUP HARD CIDER
½ cup water	Salt
	Freshly ground pepper

Melt the butter in a saucepan. Add the onion, celery and water. Boil until all the water has evaporated and the vegetables are soft. Stir in the flour and mustard until smooth. Cook over moderate heat, stirring, until the mixture froths, about 3 minutes. Stir in the cider. Simmer until thickened lightly. Season to taste with salt and pepper. Makes a big cup, I'd say.

BEER BATTER FOR FRYING FISH

Made with stale beer, this crisp batter makes enough to coat 2 pounds of fish for frying.

1 cup all-purpose flour	1 tablespoon peanut or vegetable oil
1 teaspoon baking powder	1 CUP STALE BEER
1½ teaspoons salt	Dash Tabasco

Sift the dry ingredients. Make a well in the center, add the liquids and stir until smooth.

BASIC SAUCE
RECIPES

MY SAUCE VINAIGRETTE

Quantities depend entirely on how much Vinaigrette you are going to need. Further, your taste buds are a determining factor in the seasoning. With that fixed firmly in your mind, this is what I do (largely by feel and taste).

Place *some* prepared mustard in your salad bowl. Add *some* salt and freshly ground pepper. Then add *some* wine vinegar. Beat with a wire whip until the mixture thickens somewhat and becomes cloudy. Add *some* oil (peanut or olive or half and half) and beat again. Then taste. If it lacks flavor, add some salt and/or pepper and/or mustard. Keep tasting until it tastes right. If the word "some" frightens you, start with 3 parts oil to 1 part vinegar, but rely on your taste to adjust the mixture.

As you continue to make Vinaigrette, you'll quickly learn how much of each ingredient to use.

Salvage the Mustard

When the prepared mustard jar is to all intents and purposes empty, add a tablespoon or so of vinegar. Cap and shake well. Net: a nice spot of mustard-flavored vinegar to use in salad dressings.

SAUCE BÉCHAMEL

An American cook says cream sauce and a French cook—
Sauce Béchamel. They are essentially the same thing—an
important sauce that is the basis for innumerable recipes.

The thickening agent is the *roux*—flour and fat that are
cooked together before the milk is added. I must emphasize
that it is important to cook the *roux*, otherwise it will taste
floury. The length of time you cook it depends on how it's
going to be used. If it is used immediately, in a soufflé, for
example, the *roux* need be cooked only about 3 to 4 minutes;
but if it is for a sauce, it should be cooked 6 to 8 minutes
because there is no further cooking.

The thickness of a Béchamel is in direct relation to the
proportion of flour per cup of liquid.

SAUCE	FLOUR	LIQUID
Thin sauce	1 tablespoon	1 cup
Medium Sauce	1½ tablespoons	1 cup
Thick sauce	2 tablespoons	1 cup
Heavy sauce	3 tablespoons	1 cup

The amount of fat (butter, margarine, bacon fat, goose
fat, etc.) varies according to the recipe in which the Béchamel
is being used.

To make a Béchamel: Melt the fat in a heavy saucepan
(not aluminum) over low heat. Stir in the flour until you
have a smooth paste and cook slowly, stirring constantly, until
the fat and flour froth, 3 to 4 minutes, without browning. It
should not brown unless the recipe specifically says so. Take
off the heat, add the milk and beat vigorously with a wire
whip (sometimes called whisk) to incorporate the *roux* thoroughly. Place back over a moderately high heat and cook,
still whipping, until the Béchamel comes to a boil. Boil for

1 minute, whipping constantly. Take off the heat and beat in the seasonings.

In the event the sauce must stand briefly, place a piece of plastic wrap flat on the surface to prevent a skin forming.

SAUCE VELOUTÉ

A classic sauce, Sauce Velouté is made in exactly the same way as you make a Sauce Béchamel (page 230), but the liquid is traditionally chicken broth, veal broth or fish broth instead of the milk called for in a Béchamel.

MUSTARD SAUCE

1 cup thin Sauce Béchamel
  (page 230)

1 tablespoon Dijon mustard
  or other prepared mustard

Combine the hot sauce and the mustard, mixing well. Pour into a heated serving bowl.

SAUCE MORNAY

To serve with eggs, fish, poultry, veal, vegetables, pasta or hot hors d'oeuvres.

2 cups medium Sauce
  Béchamel (page 230), or
  Sauce Velouté (page 231)
¼ to ½ cup coarsely grated
  Swiss cheese or half Swiss
  and half finely grated
  Parmesan

Salt
Freshly ground white pepper
Freshly grated nutmeg

Bring the sauce to a boil. Take off the heat, add the cheese and stir until melted. Season to taste with salt, pepper and nutmeg.

EGG SAUCE

1 cup thin Sauce Béchamel   2 hard-cooked eggs, chopped
   (page 230)

Add the eggs to the Sauce Béchamel, which is made in these proportions: 1 tablespoon butter or margarine; 1 tablespoon flour; 1 cup milk; salt and freshly ground pepper to taste.

SAUCE SUPRÊME

2 cups thick Sauce Velouté   Salt
   (page 231), made with   Freshly ground white pepper
   chicken broth   Lemon juice to taste, strained
½ cup heavy cream, about

Heat the Velouté to the simmering point. Take off the heat and beat in the cream, about 1 tablespoon at a time, until the sauce is of a light, smooth consistency. Season to taste with salt, pepper and lemon juice.

SAUCE POULETTE

1 egg yolk   1 tablespoon butter or
1½ cups medium Sauce   margarine
   Velouté (page 231)   1 tablespoon minced parsley
1 tablespoon lemon juice

Beat the egg yolk into the Sauce Velouté vigorously. Then stir in all remaining ingredients. Taste for seasoning.

OLIVE SAUCE

1 cup Brown Sauce (page 11)   Salt
1 tablespoon tomato paste   Freshly ground pepper
Dry white wine   ½ cup pitted green olives

Combine the sauce and the paste in a saucepan. Add enough dry white wine to bring the sauce to a light consistency. Taste for salt and pepper. Add the olives and bring up to a boil.

TOMATO SAUCE

If you are so fortunate as to have a garden and a surplus of tomatoes, it would behoove you to turn them into a rich sauce that you can freeze and lean on all through the winter.

3 tablespoons butter, lard, or   1½ cups meat broth (page
  bacon fat   10), heated
1 large yellow onion, peeled   ¼ teaspoon salt
  and minced   ⅛ teaspoon sugar
1 cup water   4 to 5 sprigs parsley
2 tablespoons all-purpose flour   1 small bay leaf
2 pounds ripe tomatoes,   ¼ teaspoon dried thyme
  coarsely chopped   Tomato paste (optional)

Heat the fat in a heavy saucepan. Add the onion and water. Bring to a boil. Reduce heat somewhat and cook until the onion is soft and all the water has boiled away. Stir in the flour and cook, stirring constantly, for 3 to 4 minutes. Add the tomatoes and all remaining ingredients. Bring to a boil, reduce heat and simmer for 1½ to 2 hours, skimming occasionally. Watch to see that the sauce doesn't stick to the bottom of the pan. If the sauce reduces too much add a cup or so of water. Once cooked you should have 2 to 2½ cups of a rich, fairly thick sauce.

Strain through a fine sieve, pressing with a rubber spatula to squeeze out all the juice. Taste for seasoning. If the sauce seems to lack color stir in 1 to 2 tablespoons tomato paste. Then simmer again for about 5 minutes.

To freeze, we recommend 1- or 2-cup freezer containers rather than large ones.

SAUCE DIABLE

2 tablespoons butter or
  margarine
1 medium yellow onion,
  peeled and minced
½ cup water
½ cup meat broth (page 10)
½ cup red jug wine

1 teaspoon dry mustard
2 tablespoons Worcestershire
  sauce
Salt
Freshly ground pepper
1½ teaspoons cornstarch
Dash lemon juice

Melt the butter in a heavy skillet. Add the onion and water. Boil until all the water has evaporated and the onion is soft and transparent. Stir in the broth, wine and all the seasonings. Whip in the cornstarch and cook until piping hot and slightly thickened. Just before serving stir in the lemon juice.

WHIPPED CREAM AND HORSERADISH SAUCE

½ cup heavy cream*
Juice of ½ lemon, strained
1 tablespoon prepared
  horseradish

Paprika
Salt to taste

Whip the cream until it will just hold a shape. Then fold in all remaining ingredients with a rubber spatula.

* Or ½ cup commercial sour cream.

SAUCE TARTARE

To 1 cup mayonnaise, add 1 tablespoon each of finely chopped parsley, chives, fresh tarragon, fresh chervil (if available), well-drained capers and 1 small sour pickle, finely chopped.

Serve with sautéed scallops, or poached or fried fish.

GENERAL
INFORMATION

Standard Equivalents Charts

Weights and Measures

A pinch equals as much as can be picked up between thumb and forefinger

3 teaspoons equal 1 tablespoon or ½ ounce

4 tablespoons equal ¼ cup or 2 ounces

5 tablespoons plus 1 teaspoon equal ⅓ cup

8 tablespoons equal ½ cup or 4 ounces

10 tablespoons plus 2 teaspoons equal ⅔ cup

12 tablespoons equal ¾ cup or 6 ounces

16 tablespoons equal 1 cup or 8 ounces or ½ pint

2 cups equal 1 pint or 16 ounces

2 pints equal 1 quart or 32 ounces

4 quarts equal 1 gallon

Cup Equivalents to Commercial Can Sizes

6 ounces equal ¾ cup

8 ounces equal 1 cup

10½ ounces equal 1¼ cups

13 ounces equal 1½ cups

15½ ounces equal 1¾ cups

1 pound equals 2 cups

1 pound 4 ounces equal 2½ cups

1 pound 13 ounces equal 3½ cups

2 pounds 14 ounces equal 5¾ cups

6 pounds equal 12 cups

Beans

1 pound dry white equals 2 cups uncooked / 6 cups cooked
1 pound dry kidney equals 2⅔ cups uncooked / 6¼ cooked
1 pound dry lima equals 3 cups uncooked / 7 cups cooked

Bread (Firm White)

1 slice day-old equals ¼ cup grated
1 slice fresh equals ½ cup (approximately) grated

Butter, Lard, Shortening or Margarine

1 ounce equals 2 tablespoons / ¼ stick
2 ounces equal ¼ cup / 4 tablespoons / ½ stick
4 ounces equal ½ cup / 8 tablespoons / 1 stick
½ pound equals 1 cup / 16 tablespoons / 2 sticks
1 pound equals 2 cups / 32 tablespoons / 4 sticks

Cheese

¼ pound Cheddar or Swiss, grated, equals 1 cup
¼ pound Cheddar or Swiss, in small cubes, equals ¾ cup
1 5-ounce package hard Parmesan, grated, equals 1 cup
1 3-ounce package cream cheese equals 6 tablespoons
½ pound cottage cheese equals 1 cup

Cream

½ pint heavy cream equals 1 cup / 2 cups whipped

Eggs (depending on size)

4 to 6 whole eggs equal about 1 cup
8 to 11 egg whites equal about 1 cup
12 to 14 yolks equal about 1 cup

Flour

1 pound all-purpose equals 4 cups
1 pound cake equals 4¾ to 5 cups
1 pound whole wheat equals 3½ cups

Fruits, Fresh

1 pound apples (3 medium) equals 3 cups sliced

1 pound bananas (3 medium) equals 2½ cups sliced

1 pound peaches (3 medium) equals 2 cups sliced or 1 cup mashed

1 medium lemon yields 3 tablespoons juice* / 1 tablespoon grated rind

1 lime yields about 2 tablespoons juice

1 medium orange yields about ⅓ cup juice* / 4 teaspoons grated rind

1 medium orange, peeled, yields 10 to 11 sections

1 medium grapefruit yields ⅔ cup juice*

1 medium grapefruit, peeled, yields 10 to 12 sections

1 pint box berries, except gooseberries, equals 2 cups

Fruits, Dried

1 pound prunes equals 2¾ cups / 4 cups cooked

1 pound apricots equals 3 to 3¾ cups / 4½ cups cooked

1 pound unpitted dates equals 2½ cups / 1¾ cups pitted

1 pound pitted dates equals 1¼ cups chopped

1 pound raisins equals 3 to 3¼ cups

Unflavored Gelatine

1 envelope equals 1 tablespoon.

This amount will "gel" 2 cups of liquid. (If sugar is used, it should be counted as part of the total liquid.)

Chocolate

1 ounce semisweet chocolate pieces is the equivalent of 1 ounce of any sweet cooking chocolate or 1 square, 1-ounce size, unsweetened chocolate.

---

* All citrus fruits yield more juice if dropped into boiling water for a few minutes before squeezing. However, note well, the rind *cannot* be grated after the fruit has stood in hot water.

Almonds

1 pound in shell yields 1 to 1¼ cups shelled
1 pound shelled yields 3 cups

Pecans

1 pound in shell yields 2 cups of halves / 2 cups chopped
1 pound shelled yields 4 cups

Walnuts

1 pound in shell yields 2 cups
1 pound shelled (halves) yields 4 cups

Brazil Nuts

1 pound in shell yields 1½ cups
1 pound shelled yields 3¼ cups

Peanuts

1 pound in shell yields 2 to 2½ cups
1 pound shelled yields 4 cups

Parsley

1 cup parsley sprigs equals ½ cup minced

Pasta

1 8-ounce package macaroni, noodles, or spaghetti yields 4 to
5 cups cooked
1½ cups uncooked elbow macaroni yield 3 cups cooked

Rice and Other Cereals

1 cup long grain rice equals 3 cups cooked

1 cup converted rice equals 4 cups cooked

1 cup precooked rice equals 2 cups cooked

1 cup brown rice equals 4 cups cooked

1 5-ounce package brown and wild rice equals 2 cups cooked

1 6-ounce package long grain and wild rice equals 3½ cups cooked

1 cup quick-cooking oatmeal equals 1¾ cups cooked

1 cup cornmeal equals 4 cups cooked

Sugar

1 pound granulated equals 2 to 2¼ cups

1 pound light brown, firmly packed, equals 2¼ cups

1 pound dark brown, firmly packed, equals 2½ cups

1 pound confectioners' sugar equals about 4½ cups

Vegetables

3 medium tomatoes equal 1 pound

3 medium sweet potatoes equal 1 pound / 3 cups sliced

3 medium white potatoes equal 1 pound / 2⅓ cups sliced

1 pound unshelled lima beans equals ⅔ cup shelled

1 pound unshelled peas equals 1 cup shelled

4 medium beets equal 1 pound / 2 cups diced

1 pound cabbage equals 4 cups shredded

1 medium onion equals ⅔ to 1 cup chopped

The Metric System

The metric system of measures is based on units of 10 and has been almost universally accepted because it is consistent, logical and easier to work with than our system. Your doctor uses metric measures when he writes a prescription. The can of soup you buy in the supermarket lists both ounce and gram weight; the same is true of the can of lichee nuts from Taiwan and the tin of Genovese pesto sauce from Italy. The bottle of peanut oil imported from France gives the liquid measure in ounce, quart and liter. Metrification is definitely on its way here, so it's not a moment to soon to start thinking metric.

To help you begin to familiarize yourself with the metric system, I have given you here approximate measures for both solids and liquids. In agreement with the U. S. Department of Commerce (National Bureau of Standards) I feel that we should continue to use volume measures (tablespoons and teaspoons) rather than measure such small quantities by deciliter or milliliter.

U. S. AND METRIC SYSTEMS COMPARED

Solid Measurements

Butter in Solidly Packed Standard 8-ounce Cups

2 cups equals 400 grams   ½ cup equals 100 grams
1 cup equals 200 grams   ¼ cup equals 50 grams

Granulated Sugar

1 cup equals 190 grams   ½ cup equals 95 grams
⅔ cup equals 125 grams   ¼ cup equals 50 grams

All-purpose Flour

1 cup equals 140 grams   ½ cup equals 70 grams
⅔ cup equals 100 grams   ¼ cup equals 35 grams

Rice

1 cup equals 150 grams

Liquid Measurements

2 cups equals ½ liter   ½ cup equals ⅛ liter
1 cup equals ¼ liter   ⅓ cup equals $\frac{1}{15}$ liter
¾ cup equals ⅙ liter   ¼ cup equals $\frac{1}{16}$ liter
⅔ cup equals ⅐ liter

Freezing Intelligence

GENERAL HINTS

Leftover sauce or gravy that has been refrigerated for a day or two should be brought to a boil, then chilled and frozen immediately.

Freeze leftovers in small portions. This makes it easier to determine amounts to use.

The frozen-food storage compartment in most refrigerators, those that do not have a separate door, operate at a temperature of about 15° to 20°F. They are suitable only as "everyday freezers" or short-term storage of one to two weeks. A freezer with zero (0°F.) temperature is essential to maintain quality for longer periods.

Label all packages, giving type of food, approximate number of servings and date of freezing. Do not use felt-tipped pens for your labeling because their ink washes away in a flash. Paste label on side of container rather than on top, precluding the possibility of dampness wiping out the writing.

Season sparingly as some seasonings are inclined to increase in strength during storage. Season to taste after reheating.

Cool cooked foods quickly by placing container in ice water. Then package and freeze immediately.

Do not overcook foods to be frozen. Those that must be re-heated before serving are best if only partially cooked; meat should be tender but still firm; vegetables slightly underdone.

Unsweetened fruits lose quality faster than those packed in sugar or syrup.

Use frozen foods regularly, rotating the contents of the freezer so you will have a complete and constant turnover.

PACKAGING FOOD FOR THE FREEZER

"Freezer burn" simply means drying out, and it happens because very cold air is very dry. Meat that has been exposed to air shows light gray speckled areas. Freezer burn can be prevented with moisture-proof wrapping materials that are *truly* moisture-proof.

If not properly wrapped, foods can also develop off flavors. Some types of fat (pork in particular) may get rancid if they are exposed to air—even freezer air. Smells, too, can be trans-ferred from one food to another if the food is not wrapped in airtight material. Freezer packing must be moisture-proof, vapor-proof and airtight.

Here are some of the good freezer packing materials that are available:

Substantial plastic freezer bags with closures.
Transparent plastic freezer wrap with freezer-tape or masking-tape seal.
Heavy-duty aluminum foil with tape.
Freezer meat wrap, either heavy parchment or plastic-coated stockinet to overwrap clear plastic or foil to prevent punc-tures.
Rigid plastic containers with self-sealing lids.
Freezer cartons with polyethylene liner bags and closures.

Glass containers with straight sides made especially for freezing and for easy removal.

You can substitute waxed or plastic-coated milk cartons in which to freeze soups, chili and other "loose" foods. Choose any size from a half pint to a gallon, depending on the amount of food needed for one meal. Open the top all the way across, and wash thoroughly in warm-water suds, rinse and dry. When you've refilled the carton for freezer storage, simply staple the top. The peak will allow for expansion as the food freezes. To reopen, tear the carton away from the block of food and discard.

Plastic ice-cream containers are also great for freezer use because they don't absorb tastes or odors. Do not use unless the lids snap on snugly for airtight storage.

Plastic ice-cub trays are ideal for freezing soup, gravy, broth, eggs and other liquid and semiliquid foods. Individual plastic ice-cube containers and midget containers with lids are equally satisfactory. Once frozen, whatever the container, the cubes can be removed and stored in polyethylene freezer bags, making it very easy to take just what you need for a given recipe.

Freezer wraps (plastic, freezer and heavy-duty foil) give the best possible protection when folded into the "drugstore wrap". Polyethylene bags are good for bulk foods and frozen cubes (see above).

We repeat, label and date every package. Don't rely on your memory because it is, I know, fallible!

HOW TO THAW FROZEN FOODS

Butter. If it has been frozen, should be thawed in the refrigerator.

Cheese. Frozen cheeses, wrapped, should be thawed in refrigerator and used as soon as possible after thawing. *Note:* All cheese tastes better at room temperature.

Eggs. Thaw in or out of the refrigerator. Yolks, take note, should be used immediately. Whites can be thawed, and if necessary, refrozen.

Fish and seafood. It takes 8 to 10 hours to thaw one pound of frozen fish or seafood in the refrigerator. Thaw in original package and cook immediately.

Cooked main dishes. Not necessary to thaw. Heat directly from the freezer.

Meat. Small cuts do not need thawing but you must allow one and one-half to two times the cooking time normally used. Large cuts should be thawed in the refrigerator. If thawed at room temperature the outside thaws quickly and the inside slowly, which causes loss of flavor and meat juices. Since large cuts can take up to 20 hours to thaw in the refrigerator, take them from the freezer at least the day before you plan to use them, and refrigerate.

Poultry. All thawed poultry, poultry parts and giblets must be cooked as soon as possible after thawing. Thaw in the refrigerator, still wrapped, or place in a bowl or pan under cool running water until thawed completely.

Vegetables. Frozen vegetables can be heated directly from the frozen state. Remember when heating them, they have been partially cooked and do not need the cooking time you give fresh vegetables.

Sandwiches. Thaw, still wrapped, at room temperature. Check every once in a while. Once thawed, refrigerate. Frozen sandwiches packed in a lunch box are ready to eat by noon.

Breads. For quick and yeast breads, allow to stand in unopened freezer bag at room temperature for about half an hour. If you wish to serve the bread warm take out of the bag, and place in a preheated 350° oven for 20 minutes or until warm.

Cakes. Frosted cakes should be taken from the freezer bag and thawed at room temperature. To inhibit beads of moisture forming on the frosting, use a cake cover high enough so that it does not touch the cake.

For cakes without frosting, leave wrappings intact and thaw at room temperature, or unwrap and place in a preheated 300° oven for about 10 minutes.

Baked cookies. Thaw at room temperature still in their wrappings. Unbaked cookie dough frozen in a roll should be sliced, placed on a cookie sheet and baked according to recipe directions.

Pies. Thaw baked pies, unopened, at room temperature. If the pies are usually served warm remove wrapping and place in a preheated 350° oven for about 20 minutes.

Unbaked pies should be unwrapped, the top crust brushed with milk or egg white, slit in a couple of places to allow steam to escape, then baked according to recipe directions.

Thaw *unbaked pastry* at room temperature. Shape and use as you would fresh.

Whipped cream. Take from freezer and place in refrigerator for about half an hour. Spoon on dessert or whatever and return to refrigerator.

Canapés and hors d'oeuvres. About noon of the day you plan to serve them, take from the container and arrange in single layers on serving trays. Cover loosely with plastic wrap or waxed paper and thaw in the refrigerator.

Nuts, shelled or unshelled. If stored in quilted freezer bags and frozen they keep their fresh flavor almost indefinitely. They defrost in a very short time, 10 to 15 minutes.

DO NOT FREEZE

Milk and unwhipped cream. They don't come out of the freezer as appetizing as they went in. Freeze in an emergency only.

Buttermilk, sour cream, yoghurt and similar milk products. Freezing and thawing change their smooth texture.

Creamed cottage cheese. It gets mushy and unappetizing. Freeze only uncreamed or dry-curd cottage cheese.

Eggs in the shell. They will expand and crack the shell. Break into individual ice-cube containers. Ideally, one whole egg fits in each mold with room to expand.

Hard-cooked eggs. The whites get tough and rubbery.

Fully cooked fried foods. Apt to be soggy. Undercook, then freeze. However, I've had good luck with potato croquettes that I've frozen, then reheated in the oven from the frozen state.

Cooked macaroni, spaghetti and noodles. They are inclined to get mushy when reheated after freezing.

Seasoned meat. Some seasonings become stronger; others get weaker.

Home-prepared stuffed poultry. Raw or cooked, it can develop harmful bacteria that can cause serious illness. Freeze the bird unstuffed, then stuff when you are ready to cook. Remove dressing from cooked poultry and freeze in a separate container. *Note:* Commercially frozen stuffed poultry is safe for freezer storage because the packer uses special processing techniques to prepare the stuffing.

Giblets. Hearts, liver and other in-meats should be packaged separately because their storage life is short. Further, you use them differently in many instances.

Unblanched vegetables. If frozen unblanched they not only lose their color but their nutritional value.

Fresh, whole tomatoes. They will collapse during thawing because of their high water content.

Raw potatoes. Raw potatoes get mushy after freezing. Cook until almost done, then freeze. Boiled potatoes get watery and tough, but you can freeze them when they are baked or mashed.

Potato salad. Made with boiled potatoes, mayonnaise and hard-cooked eggs—all unfreezable ingredients.

Sandwiches made with uncooked vegetables such as lettuce, celery, radishes, carrots and with mayonnaise. The vegetables get limp and the mayonnaise separates. See however, lettuce soup (page 168), celery tops (page 158), etc.

Meringues. Off or on a pie, they get watery during thawing and will no longer hold their peaks.

Unbaked batter or yeast dough. The quality isn't as good and the time saved doesn't amount to much, if any. Better to bake, then freeze.

Custard pies. After thawing, they're watery, tough and unappetizing.

Layer cakes with soft fillings. The filling makes the thawed cake soggy. Bake and freeze the layers separately and fill when thawed.

Egg-white frostings. They don't hold up through freezing and thawing. However, butter and fudge-type frostings will freeze.

Cracker canapés. Crackers get soft and limp after freezing. Freeze the spreads only and spread on fresh, crisp crackers at serving time.

INDEX

About the Author

Helen McCully is one of the most distinguished food experts in the country. She is the Food Editor of *House Beautiful,* where she has two monthly columns and a monthly food feature. She was, for many years, the Food Editor of *McCall's* and has appeared frequently on radio and television. She lives in New York City.